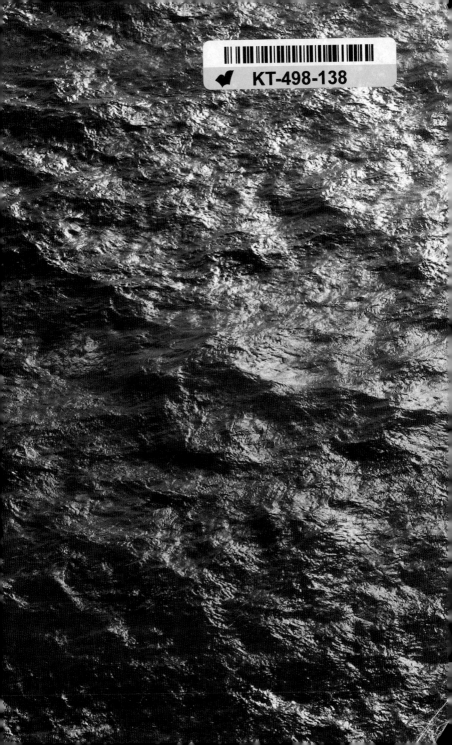

RACE
AGAINST
TIME

RACE AGAINST TIME

ELLEN MACARTHUR

PENGUIN BOOKS

PENGUIN BOOKS

Published by the Penguin Group
Penguin Books Ltd, 80 Strand, London WC2R 0RL, England
Penguin Group (USA) Inc., 375 Hudson Street, New York, New York 10014, USA
Penguin Group (Canada), 90 Eglinton Avenue East, Suite 700, Toronto, Ontario, Canada M4P 2Y3
(a division of Pearson Penguin Canada Inc.)
Penguin Ireland, 25 St Stephen's Green, Dublin 2, Ireland (a division of Penguin Books Ltd)
Penguin Group (Australia), 250 Camberwell Road, Camberwell, Victoria 3124, Australia
(a division of Pearson Australia Group Pty Ltd)
Penguin Books India Pvt Ltd, 11 Community Centre, Panchsheel Park, New Delhi – 110 017, India
Penguin Group (NZ), cnr Airborne and Rosedale Roads, Albany, Auckland 1310, New Zealand
(a division of Pearson New Zealand Ltd)
Penguin Books (South Africa) (Pty) Ltd, 24 Sturdee Avenue, Rosebank, Johannesburg 2196, South Africa

Penguin Books Ltd, Registered Offices: 80 Strand, London WC2R 0RL, England

www.penguin.com

First published by Michael Joseph 2005
Published in Penguin Books 2006
1

The picture acknowledgements on page 286 constitute an extension of this copyright page

Typeset by Rowland Phototypesetting Ltd, Bury St Edmunds, Suffolk
Printed in Italy by Printer Trento S.r.L.

ISBN-13: 978-0-141-02648-0
ISBN-10: 0-141-02648-0

I dedicate this book to the whole team – the best team in the world. You know who you are. Few people really understand what it took to make this happen – you really do. Thank you.

ellen x

CONTENTS

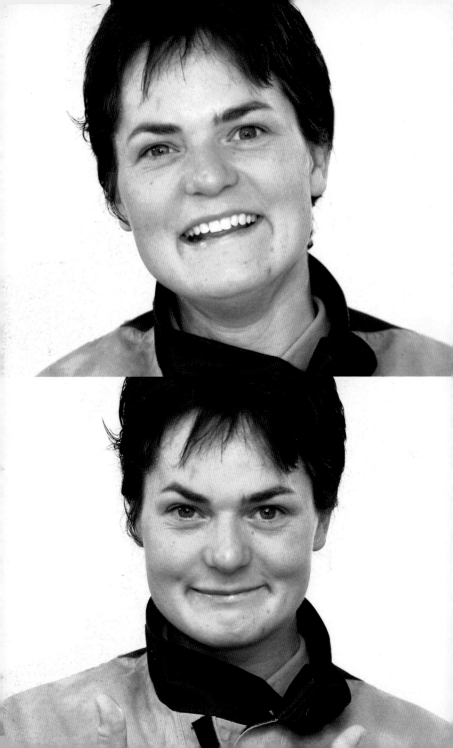

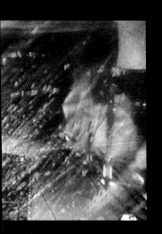

INTRODUCTION

Imagine driving a car, fast, off-road at night in lashing rain. You're forced to hang on to the steering wheel just to stay in your seat, and you have no idea what's coming next, as you have no headlights. To make matters worse, you have no windscreen wipers clearing your view. In fact, you have no windscreen. No roof. That's how it feels sailing fast in the Southern Ocean at night.

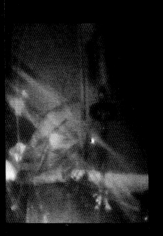
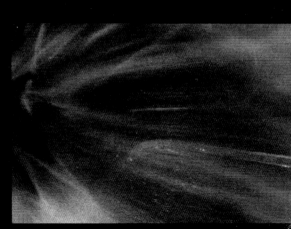

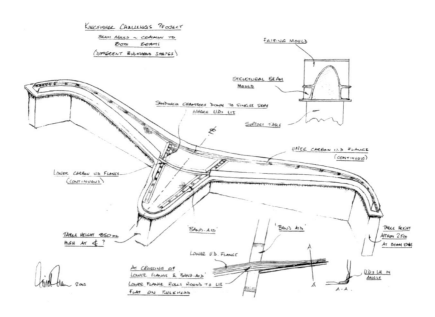

KINGFISHER CHALLENGE PROJECT
BEAM MOULD — COMMON TO
BOTH BEAMS
(DIFFERENT BULKHEAD SHAPES)

FAIRING MOULD

STRUCTURAL BEAM MOULD

SANDWICH CHAMFERS DOWN TO SINGLE SKIN
WHERE U.D.s LIT

SUPPORT TABLE

UPPER CARBON U.D. FLANGE
(CONTINUOUS)

LOWER CARBON U.D FLANGE
(CONTINUOUS)

TABLE HEIGHT 850mm
HIGH AT ℄ ?

'BAND-AID'

'BAND AID'

TABLE HEIGHT
APPROX 2500
AT BEAM ENDS

LOWER U.D. FLANGE

U.D.s LIE IN ANGLE

AT CROSSING OF
LOWER FLANGE & BAND-AID
LOWER FLANGE ROLLS ROUND TO LIE
FLAT ON BULKHEAD

A-A.

It's not necessarily difficult to be on a boat in those conditions. It's like a fairground ride: it can be a thrill, and parts of it can be fun. But when you're on the fairground ride day after day, night after night, without respite, it becomes harder and harder to deal with. You're out there to push hard, and if you don't, you don't stand a chance of breaking a record. There's always an unsettling feeling of nervousness, mixed up with stress and fatigue. You can't switch off; it eats away at you, bit by bit. Lots of wind, and there is a very real risk that the boat can capsize; no wind, and you're petrified that you won't break the record.

You try to sleep by curling up in a ball between the cockpit and the inside of the boat – there's only the impression of warmth that comes from the red glow of the instruments. You close your eyes, and sometimes, to get warmer, pull a piece of

NIGEL IRENS DESIGN

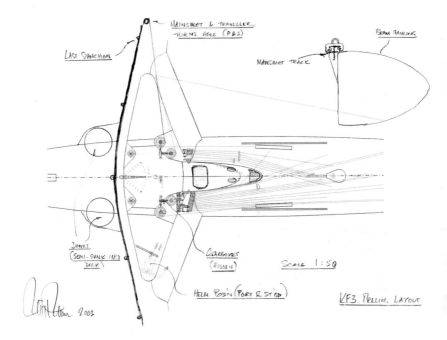

LAST STANCHION

MAINSHEET & TRAVELLER
TURNS HERE (PRS)

BEAM FAIRING

MAINSHEET TRACK

DONES
(SEMI-SUNK INTO DECK)

GEARBOXES
(HIDDEN)

SCALE 1:50

HELM POS'N (PORT R ST'BD)

VF3 PRELIM. LAYOUT

2003

fleece right up over your oilskins until it covers your face. You may be exhausted, *absolutely* exhausted . . . but if you hear just a tiny creak that isn't normal, no matter where it is, you get to your feet once more to investigate. When your eyes close, you never know how long it will be for. You never know if you will even fall asleep. Your life revolves around keeping the boat pumping, keeping her singing, keeping her breathing . . . without breaking anything. Not just for hours, days or weeks, but for *months*.

You're on the edge 24/7. Inside you, the nervousness is always there, nagging away. It's like the feeling you have before you go to the dentist, or if you have an exam that day. You find it hard to have normal conversations with people; you don't really feel like eating. It's a feeling that rarely left me on this trip, and day by day it chipped away at my reserves.

For the first time in my life I knew that I was going, mentally and physically, further than was actually safe for me. I was right on the edge – of fatigue, of my body's capabilities and even perhaps of logic. Sleep deprivation has been used as torture, and there is no doubt that it is the single hardest thing to deal with out there. You can train hard in a gym to be strong, you can prepare yourself in every way to be ready, but you cannot control the weather, or successfully prevent its debilitating effect on your well-being. And then there's the clock: in a record attempt, you are racing against it, and it doesn't have bad days. It doesn't suffer from light winds or from breakages – that's the hardest and most relentless thing about it.

As a kid I had dreamt of sailing solo around the world; I had dreamt of the adventure, the ocean, the challenges and the knowledge. I have always loved

learning, and I feel that I learn each time I set foot on a boat – that in itself is a huge motivation to get out there.

Before this attempt I had already sailed once around the world, and during that journey I was alone at sea for just over three months. It had been incredibly hard in the Vendée to cope with the sleep deprivation, the stress and the breakages, but this trip was so much harder. *B&Q* is a 75-foot trimaran, which puts her in a different class from the other boats that I've raced, like the Open 60s. Multihulls also live on the edge. They fly over the water, rather than sail through it. I was unbelievably nervous when I left, feeling like I just wanted the hours to pass so that I could get across that line. I knew inside that I was going to be tested like never before, and I was right.

During the Vendée I found a little time to relax, to reflect and to take in quite a lot of what was around me. On this trip it was very different. The pleasure was more limited; it was a different experience. Physically there was no help. There were no electric or hydraulic winches – everything on *B&Q* is done manually. It's tough when you're pulling sails that are three times your own body weight up the mast; even tougher when you're doing it several times a day. But I couldn't let that stop me.

In something like the Vendée you are racing the other competitors around you. Everyone is affected by similar weather patterns, which means that even when there is no wind you're able to take miles from your competitors by sailing well. This time, there was only the clock. Always ticking. It's merciless.

I knew before I embarked on the round-the-world record attempt that it would be harder than I could imagine. When *B&Q* went into the water in December 2003 the record stood at just over ninety-three

As a kid I had dreamt of sailing solo around the world; I had dreamt of the adventure, the ocean, the challenges and the knowledge

days, but within weeks of her launch that record had been slashed by over twenty days by a Frenchman called Francis Joyon. This not only made Francis a national hero in France, but also one of the two people in history who had made it solo, non-stop round the world in a multihull. Many thought that Francis's record would stand for years – maybe even I did, inside – but none the less, on 28 November 2004, I set out on my first attempt to break the record. Although I tried to pace myself at the beginning of the trip, I soon realized that this wasn't an option. I really had to get on with it, so I started to push hard from the outset and then continued without let-up.

But it wasn't just me. Though the majority of what you see within these pages describes one person's struggle over seventy-one days, it doesn't perhaps really reflect just how much of a team effort this project has been. A *team* of people devoted themselves to it with commitment, energy and passion over a period of two years. And we always knew that however hard it got, we were doing what we wanted to do. We alone had the responsibility for setting ourselves such a daunting challenge.

It is still hard to believe that we did actually break the record – in some ways the whole thing has felt a bit like a dream. From the first moments – when we announced B&Q's sponsorship, when Nigel Irens began to sketch boat designs, and even when the huge scale of *B&Q* (affectionately known as Mobi) became apparent as she took shape in an Australian boat yard – the project has seemed unreal, with some parts incredible and some more like nightmares . . . The trip was amazing, and it made me feel alive, but, looking back on the whole project, I think that the most fantastic moments have been those that I've been able to share with the team: both the immediate team that I work with, and those who made such a massive difference by supporting us over the internet, and through letters and e-mails.

When I crossed that finish line on 7 February, I felt little emotion other than relief. It was only when the team jumped on board an hour later that I really experienced the most incredible joy and excitement. I have never believed that this was 'my record'. It's very definitely 'our record'.

And that was the moment we were first able to celebrate it. However long it lasts, I shall always remember it that way.

I saw some incredible things in those seventy-one days at sea, and I've tried to gather those images together here so that the drama, colour and vastness of offshore and single-handed sailing could be brought to life in as visual and direct a way as possible. But this book is not an attempt to reflect on the record. It is a raw, harsh and direct account of what was the hardest thing I have ever been through by far. It's an account of day-to-day life on a boat that is ploughing relentlessly through the oceans. And, while I tried not to make the book too technical, to a certain extent it had to be in order to convey how a mind is forced to function when pushing hard at sea. It has not been rewritten, softened or polished – it is simply 'our story' as it was, and I hope that it does not seem on occasions to be too negative or uncomfortable a read. The time will come when I will be able to reflect on this voyage and bring some perspective to it, but what follows is as intimate and immediate a record of our race around the world as there is ever likely to be.

DAY ONE 28/11/04
B&Q crosses the start line at 08:10:44

Well, here we are, out on the open ocean once more ... It's going to be a tough one, this ... I can feel it, and really know that I'm going to have to dig very, very deep ... The most important thing, though, which I keep hammering into the front of my mind, is that I really want to enjoy this. *B&Q* is the most unbelievable boat, and she has such an incredible feeling about her – I just really, really want to do the voyage justice for her too. I'm sitting here, obviously alone, and in fact feeling very, very nervous. We're off – and the Omega clock I can see right next to me is very definitely ticking ... How hard do we push, how gingerly do we sail, how much will *B&Q* take, how much will I take? These are all things which right now are in the front of my mind. I just hope that I'll be able to relax into this, and appreciate it for what it is ... better go – I can feel a genoa-to-solent change coming on ...

x

We're off – and the clock I can see right next to me is very definitely ticking

B&Q is the most unbelievable boat, and she has such an incredible feeling about her – I want to do the voyage justice for her too

Back again – changed sails in a rather full cockpit, since I'd dragged the sails back there . . . I noticed a few fantastic things as we left . . . There was an unbelievable stillness as we left the dock – funny, as if no one really wanted to make too much noise – all very odd . . . But it was fantastic to feel the atmosphere there. Falmouth gave us all an outstanding send-off – I'm overwhelmed ... really overwhelmed. It all seemed a bit like a dream . . . As we were towed out of the harbour there was a cormorant diving on our bows, and just a few hours later, as we sailed out of the harbour entrance, we had dolphins swimming around us . . . magnificent . . .

Time for a quick nap now . . .

x

DAY TWO 29/11/04
1 hour 58 minutes behind
120 miles from Cape Finisterre

I've decided not to push too hard just yet and to be conservative. We're sailing with one reef and the genoa at the moment. Got a lot of sleep (2.5 hours!) for the first time last night, but I don't feel great right now. I'm still pretty nervous; I think that's going to take a few days to wear off and will probably return at times during the trip. But it's very good to be out here, it's good to be sailing the boat, it's good to be thinking about the weather patterns ahead and the hurdles we have to face over the next few days – all of that takes away some of the impact of knowing you're going to be at sea for over two months. Had a bit of a drama yesterday evening: just before midnight the main rudder cassette box flipped up and broke

I'm still pretty nervous; I think that's going to take a few days to wear off and will probably return at times during the trip

two of the fuses. I heard a noise, though I couldn't work out what it was. I went all over the boat but couldn't see anything, and then there was another noise a couple of hours later and that's when I saw that the box had kicked up. What I think may actually have happened was that during the big, violent waves at the beginning, the rudder was hit hard enough to loosen it and the fuses were stretched a little bit. Then, just as we were sailing along, both fuses bust. Replacing them was a pain-in-the-arse job! They seem to be OK now, though.

Went through the ridge of the high last night. We're on the latitude of Finisterre and sailing into this depression now, so it's a bit windier and the sea is getting bigger. It's warmed up a little; we've got a breeze at the moment coming from the east. There's bright sunshine today with very few scattered white clouds. It's actually very nice sailing, but the sea conditions aren't very pleasant. It's quite rough, and with this wind speed we're piling into the waves ahead regularly. The breeze didn't go as light as we thought it would overnight; our average speed went down quite a lot – two hours at 17 knots, a couple at 15, so a bit rubbish – but we appear to be off again.

> **Progress seems to be a little slower than we'd hoped. But the breeze is much better now – that's a good sign**

DAY THREE 30/11/04
7 minutes ahead
230 miles off Lisbon

We are currently just on top of a low-pressure system between the Spanish and Portuguese coasts.

I've had a pretty frustrating night. The sea was terrible; there was a really bad cross swell. *B&Q*'s uncomfortable with waves coming from the east side of the depression ahead. There were quite light winds, and we've been trying to get between the low pressure and the high, but, unfortunately, we haven't been able to manage to do that as quickly as we wanted. So progress seems to be a little slower than we'd hoped. But the breeze is much better now – 18 knots and sailing normally again, so that's a good sign. I've still not got the gennaker up. We're crashing around too much, and it would only have been for a few hours anyway.

Right now I can see a huge cloud with me – a real monster. We'll be heading into a low and into high winds soon. Speeds should be over 40 knots, the highest wind speeds we've had so far, so it'll be pretty tough sailing.

The unstable sea state has stressed me out a lot. Right from the beginning every decision has been critical; each day counts. I'm pretty much neck and neck with Francis at the moment, but the trip down to the Equator could change that. I'm looking forward to settling into life on board, and I'll be glad to see the back of the low in the next twenty-four hours. And in a couple of days' time we'll be in the Trade Winds heading down to the Equator, so, all being well, it'll be a little bit more restful.

DAY FOUR 1/12/04
3 hours 5 minutes ahead
Passes Madeira

The wind is all over the place at the moment – it's suddenly shifted through 120 degrees, which is making me very nervous. It's just in the clouds; it shouldn't be like this. The breeze is due to die, but, until I can get out of this cloud mass, nothing's going to change. It's gone from 8 knots to 25, and that makes it very hard on board. It's not good for our positioning on the Canary Islands ahead of us. Right now our boat speed is just 8 knots, and

I'm heading for the islands. I can't leave the boat for five minutes without something happening. I hope it's going to stabilize soon.

I have a very dry mouth, and I'm not eating properly yet. I've not totally got my head into this. I'm going to try to fix the leak on the fresh-water tank to make myself feel happier! Problem is that with the wind shifting all the time, I don't want to get stuck down below, as I keep having to rush on deck to trim the sheets.

DAY FIVE 2/12/04
57 minutes ahead
130 miles south-west of the Canary group

We had relatively stable conditions last night, but the wind was slightly up and down. I got more sleep last night than I'd had in the previous few days. The past two days have been very, very difficult. Yesterday was supposed to be a relaxing day, as the breeze was going to kick in from the north, but that just didn't happen. We ended up with a very, very changeable wind, and it was extremely tiring just keeping the boat going to make it round the Canary Islands. But yesterday afternoon the wind was up and down so much, I felt like I'd never be able to get the boat moving again. Today things are much better and I'm much happier. We have 20 knots of breeze right now, and I'm surfing between 16 and 22 knots, which is fantastic. The depression has been here for a while, so the sea has just built and built, and occasionally we hit a wave very hard. The goal for the rest of the day is to stay in the breeze and south of the high.

DAY SIX 3/12/04
2 hours 30 minutes behind
450 miles off the African coast

I've felt under immense pressure since leaving – the pressure of that clock that never stops, and those minutes that never stop flowing

I had a very fast night, with 15 to 18 knots of breeze, but now the wind direction has gone completely ballistic. I think it's to do with the clouds so I'm going to keep the gennaker up for a while. There have been a lot of clouds, and this has made things significantly slower. I felt nervous this morning, but I think that happens after some good sleep, and a bit of dreaming! Day Six breakfast is porridge: there are a couple of apples left, but they are going brown now because we are at 20 degrees north and the boat is hot, so everything is getting quite warm – I didn't anticipate being so far south so quickly. It's not the most comfortable place to be!

At the moment we're sailing pretty much in the Trade Winds. We're between the Canaries and the Cape Verdes, so we're sailing with wind from the east, with gennaker and full main like we were all day yesterday and the two previous nights. It's relatively calm on board. It's OK until we get a gust and then we have to be very careful not to have too much load in the sails. It's a case of always being vigilant and ready to ease out the lines. There's been a lot of up and down out of the cockpit, being ready to ease things when the wind increases. We haven't had any really big squall clouds yet, but they're on the way – I can see them on the horizon. It's going to be a pretty tough few days coming up to the Equator.

I spent a long time going over Francis's positions and his average speeds and things. I needed to get a grip on that, as I think we're going to have a slow approach to the Doldrums which lie a few hundred miles to the north of the Equator. I noticed that on his way back up the Atlantic, Francis averaged only 11 knots over a ten-day period, which makes me feel better!

We've had a bit of an issue with the rudder cassette box. We got hit pretty hard by a wave at Ushant, and it seemed to make the box move slightly in its case. I've sailed 25,000 miles with this in situ and it's been absolutely fine, but now it wants to play up – we've still got about 1 mm of movement in the box. Yesterday I lifted the box completely out of the water. I slowed down, pulled up the rudder, checked it all out – there are no serious problems. It's mainly just the fact that it's wobbling a bit. I had the rudder out of the water for about forty-five minutes. We probably didn't lose too much boat speed – we were still moving about 8 or 9 knots during that period, so it probably cost us about five miles, which isn't too bad at this stage. It was good to lift it up to see what the situation was and to actually check it out properly. I've made some wedges and they're all in place now, so we're going to monitor its progress as we head south.

Well, I think that last night was my first real sleep since leaving a few days ago – and, though I felt pretty groggy as the sun came up, I knew that it had been very, very necessary. Trying to sleep on poor *B&Q*, who is relentlessly powering through the oceans, is far from easy – this was never going to be an easy record to break. Just in the past few days I think I've realized what the scale of the task actually is ... I've felt under immense pressure since leaving – the pressure of that clock that never stops, and those minutes that never stop flowing. I've felt nervous, and tired, and generally pretty damn stressed since we left too. I've rarely felt any sign of hunger – though luckily have been doing this long enough now to know that I just need to eat anyway – and I've done that.

That's one part of me that is working correctly and that's a start at least!

We've had our fair share of problems since leaving, ranging from leaks in the water system to a dangerous creaking noise from the rudders. Some frighten the life out of you and others just make you realize that the list of things out here never, ever stops. Each problem is just a few more grams of your energy gently sapping away ...

The big storm we just went through was good for me, I think, as it made me go into 'survival mode', into the 'just-get-to-the-other-side mode', which at least stopped me thinking about all the stressful things. There's nothing like a gust over 45 knots to focus the mind on what is important in that moment!

But today, while hanging off the back of the boat, lifting the main rudder out of the water, I was taken up sharp. I had my head in the rudder cassette box, looking for damage in the case, but, as I looked down, I saw a mesmerizing flow of bright blue water flying beneath her hull. It was such a contrast to the stressful hour of slowing the boat down for repairs that I smiled out loud (if you can do that!) and leant down to touch this beautiful miracle of life. Just water – but in that second it was priceless ...

So, time for bed now. I need to sleep as much as I possibly can, as the weather is relatively stable. Having said that, though, the winds have been up to 25 knots and down to 16 since I've been typing this mail ...
Later then

DAY SEVEN 4/12/04
3 hours 8 minutes ahead
112 miles south-west of the
Cape Verde Islands

Things on board are pretty good, although it's very hot now. We're at 14 degrees north, so we're getting down towards the Equator. But I feel more relaxed than I did to begin with. There's still a massive amount of tension, and obviously I still want to do very well and am giving my absolute maximum. Conditions are more stable, so I've been able to do a lot of checks on the boat, wander around inspecting things, change a few lashings, make a few finishing touches. So things generally feel OK on board, but it is stressful. You spend most of your time waiting or thinking what's going to break next, and it's not particularly healthy for the brain. But we're doing OK. I'm more relaxed than I was at the beginning, which is a good sign.

I think at the beginning things were difficult because we had quite changeable conditions that made for a very stressful start, but it's nice to be down in the Trade Winds now. The boat's performing fantastically. I'm so pleased with her speed. She's really amazing, which is great to see. She feels pretty safe as well, even in the squalls, which is good. I know that we're going to have a difficult Doldrums crossing, but right now our speed's good and we've gained a few hours' lead on Francis.

He had a very good Doldrums crossing because the Trade Winds were strong to the north. We've got weaker Trade Winds, which means it's going to be harder for us. Rather than having weather systems like those in the northern and southern hemispheres, the Doldrums are literally the gap between them. There are no highs and no lows, really, it's just a whole load of clouds forming because the water's so hot. It's a very difficult region to cross, and you can get it good and you can get it bad. It doesn't look like we're going to have one of the best crossings, but we'll see what happens.

Sleep is one of the most important things we can possibly have. We forget in day-to-day life just how important it is

DAY EIGHT 5/12/04
13 hours 16 minutes ahead
500 miles north of the Equator

We're just over a week in now, so it's still very early days. We've completed about 10 per cent, but we've had our fair share of issues already. There have been a few worries, a few things that have needed checking. The movement in the rudder was certainly a huge issue, although it seems like it might be all right. There have been all sorts of things going on, really. And, as I imagined, it's been pretty hard. But we've been lucky with the conditions over the last few days, very lucky with the breeze. We've still got 10–11 knots from the east, so we're making due south at the moment at about 14–15 knots, which is a pretty good speed at which to be tackling the Doldrums area. The boat now seems great – no major problems. Just been doing a few bits and pieces on board, monitoring things and making sure everything is ready for the Southern Ocean, which seems unbelievably close in a strange way. I've also been looking at the weather to see what we're going to be facing in the South Atlantic.

Things have been OK going through the Doldrums so far, but we're not through yet. The Doldrums can go either way. It's a little bit the luck of the cards that you're dealt on the day, but, at the moment, touch wood, we seem OK. We're still at 7 degrees north, and things seem all right at the moment, but anything can change – it all depends on what the next conditions are. The latest satellite picture shows that right now we're in a fantastic clear blue area, but to the south of us there are a lot of clouds and I'm hoping they're going to move away to the west in the next few hours so we can pass through without too many problems.

It's unbelievably hot now. It's good to be on a multihull, because you're moving quickly and you've got a nice breeze over the deck, but it's still very hot and humid. The temperature inside the cabin is around 32 degrees during the day and 29 at night – it takes a lot of your energy away. I've been sleeping in the cuddy on a beanbag on the outside of the boat – I think I've only slept on the bunk on the inside twice since the start. You feel more comfortable out there, closer to the boat and closer to the ropes. I'm trying to recover as much as possible so that when we go into the South Atlantic and the changeable conditions, I'm as rested as I can be, because sleep is one of the most important things we can possibly have. We forget in day-to-day life just how important it is – and until you're lacking it, you don't realize what a luxury it can be!

DAY NINE 6/12/04
8 hours 27 minutes ahead
245 miles from the Equator

I'm tired this morning; the Doldrums were pretty bad during the night.

I think on the whole we got away with passing through without too many problems, but, all the same, last night was really tough. The wind was going from 4 knots one minute to 20 knots the next. I didn't get any sleep at all during the day yesterday, as there were lots of sail changes and other things going on. It's been very hard, because you desperately have to keep the boat moving no matter what – moving is the only way to get to the new breeze you're looking for. The sky is full of huge great big black clouds and there is no moon at the moment, which is even worse, as it's very hard to see what's coming. You're

constantly battered by squalls and rain in the clouds. One minute you've suddenly got 5 knots of wind, and you need a completely different amount of sails than you do for 20 knots of breeze heading in the same direction. I must have changed sails about six or seven times during the night and goodness knows how many times during the day yesterday. It's a constant fight to have the right amount of sails to keep the boat moving without breaking anything, which isn't very easy to do when you're suddenly getting such aggressive squalls.

It was good to feel that steady breeze again from the south-east this morning, and there's no reason we should slow down now. We've got 15 knots of breeze and are making pretty good progress, but we're not going particularly fast because we're upwind. It'll be good when we can crack off a bit and go a little bit faster, but for the moment we're hanging in there. We're happy with our current position, although it would be nice to be a bit further east, but I'm not sure we would have had the same crossing through the Doldrums area if we had been. If this breeze stays with us, and there's no reason it shouldn't, then we should cross the Equator before Francis, which would be awesome.

Physically I'm OK, but I'm losing a lot of fluids. I'm trying to drink a huge amount because it's just so warm on board, particularly when I'm charging the batteries – the cabin turns into even more of an oven, more like a sauna! There's no escape from it; there's nowhere to go. All the water around you is salty, you're salty, and so your sweat is salty! I've got lots of salt sores all over my hands and my arms, which appear when you are sweaty for long periods of time. It's pretty difficult, but you've just got to think ahead and know that it's going to be getting colder soon, which is a negative thing but also a positive one too.

I'm looking forward to getting across and into the south, I really am. At the moment we've got a pretty good course and we're heading almost south. The Equator is roughly 200 miles away, so I reckon we should be crossing, all being well, in about twelve hours – about midnight tonight, English time. We should keep the breeze until we get there. In time, as we head south, the wind will turn more to the east, and we'll be able to sail faster along the coast of Brazil before plunging down round the high pressure of the St Helena high and into the Southern Ocean.

You desperately have to keep the boat moving no matter what – moving is the only way to get to the new breeze you're looking for

Just a quick mail from the equatorial area ... *B&Q* is sailing along like a dream, and all OK on board. It's now very, very hot on board, and, though I'm still in my thermals at night, I'm not sure that they're really necessary. The night-time cabin temp is 29 degrees – and the day-time one higher. As well as the sores on my hands, any tiny scratch appears to become infected – better watch out. But hopefully in a few more days things will start to calm down, just better not forget that I'm leaving summer and sailing into winter, though! Better go, time to send this,

from a slightly nervous but happy ellen x

Every sailor always gives a gift to Neptune at the Equator. I opened a bottle of champagne to celebrate the moment

DAY TEN 7/12/04
10 hours 31 minutes ahead
Fastest solo time to the Equator

We've set a new solo Ushant-to-Equator time of 8 days, 18 hours and 20 minutes, taking 14 hours and 3 minutes off the previous time set by Francis Joyon.

Every sailor always gives a gift to Neptune – he is always around us at sea, and a mark of respect is always shown at the Equator. So I gave a copy of Lance Armstrong's book to Neptune, and I also opened a very small bottle of champagne to celebrate the moment. It was pretty cool to know that we'd actually crossed; it's always quite a big moment in a round-the-world trip. It's our first milestone – here's to the next one . . . and to the south!

I've got quite a few bottles of champagne on board: one for the Equator on the way down, one for the Cape of Good Hope, one for Cape Leeuwin underneath Australia, one for Cape Horn and then one for the Equator on the way back up. These bottles mark the most important days in the record – the days when Mobi and I cross the major capes or the Equator. These are big moments for us, and I guess therefore we celebrate them to comply with tradition.

It's fantastic to be ahead of the record, and good for the motivation, but we know it's still very early days, and although it's a good feeling to be ahead and cruising south with good breeze, it's also a moment when you know it's just one of the milestones and a lot could

**The visit by the navy
was incredible. I felt
really emotional once
they had gone; they
made Mobi and me
feel very special!**

change between now and later, there's
no doubt about it. I've always imagined
this trip in five sections: the first going
down to the Equator, the second going
down to the Southern Ocean, the third
the Southern Ocean itself, the fourth
back up to the Equator and the fifth the
Equator to home. The first two are about
ten days each, the third one is about
thirty days and the last two are about ten
days each. We've ticked off one of those
ten-day boxes, and we're probably about
a seventh of the way through. But my
eyes are very firmly focused on the days
ahead: first of all finding somewhere that
is a little bit cooler than where we are
now but also plunging down into the
Southern Ocean.

The visit by the navy was incredible.
Just a few hours before I crossed the
Equator, I was joined by two ships: there

was the Royal Fleet Auxiliary vessel *Gold
Rover* and the Royal Navy's HMS *Iron
Duke*. The first thing I saw was the
helicopter they had sent out to buzz the
boat. We spoke for a while on the radio.
I told them I wouldn't be home for
Christmas or New Year, but they said
I shouldn't worry as I'd be back for
Valentine's Day! It was very, very odd to
have human contact after a week without
seeing anyone or anything, really. They
stayed with me for about an hour and just
before leaving the ships' company came
on deck to cheer and wave. It was an
incredible feeling – this has never
happened to me before! I chatted with the
captain for a while, then they peeled away,
one from my port side and one from my
starboard, and carried on their way home.
I felt really emotional once they had gone;
they made Mobi and me feel very special!

At the moment it's looking like there may be a corridor between the St Helena high pressure and the low pressure developing off the Brazilian coast. It's actually going to be quite difficult to sit between the high and the low, because if we go too far south, behind the front of the low, the sea conditions will be terrible and there will be no wind. If we go to the north, into the high, we'll lose the wind completely and we won't be able to stay in the gap. Timing is going to be absolutely crucial. It may pay off, it may not, but we don't really have any choice – we've got to go through that gap and we've got to hope we make it. We're going to have to be sailing as fast as we possibly can in order to get through the gap that will spit us out into the Southern Ocean.

There's no guarantee that we'll have the same weather as Francis, so we could very easily lose all the time we've pulled ahead so far. We could gain some, we could lose some, it can move both ways. I think one thing that was very clear when we set off was that Francis had had a very good run down the Atlantic, and down the South Atlantic too. It's great to be this far ahead of him at the Equator, but for him the South Atlantic was pretty good, so we'll have to see how that goes and how we go into the Southern Ocean. The next big landmark, I think, will be going underneath the Cape of Good Hope down into the Southern Ocean – that really symbolizes that you're down in the cold south. We'll be surfing the waves of the Southern Ocean for approximately one month and it's going to be a challenging time. I'm very nervous, but I'm looking forward to it.

DAY ELEVEN 8/12/04
12 hours 31 minutes ahead
270 miles ENE of Cape Recife

I've been trying to sleep in the cuddy – it's getting slightly cooler now at 29 degrees, after 35, which was stifling. The road into the Southern Ocean looks really bad. I've discussed this with Commanders – our weather routers in the States – and it looks like we're going to have to go upwind to get there. There's a real risk of getting stuck in the middle of the high pressure of the St Helena anticyclone if we try to ride across it. I know it's going to be mentally and physically exhausting, with a lot of sail changes needed to get across, so I'm trying to sleep and eat as much as possible – even managed a two-hour sleep last night. We're approaching a part where Francis was very fast, averaging 19 knots. I've been trying to manage my own expectations of the next

Our conditions are worse than the ones Francis had, and we're just going to have to do the best we can with them. We know we're going to have a rough time

few days – saying that, thinking about it, has stressed me, making it even harder to sleep!

At the moment we're in the South Atlantic Trade Winds, and we've got a good breeze that has been relatively steady for the last couple of days. But within thirty-six hours that's going to change. We're going to have the wind back on us, as a result of the depression that's forming off the Brazilian coast. Shortly after that, this depression is going to move east, and we're not going to be able to stay with it. It will probably disappear into the high-pressure system, and if we try to follow it we're going to get eaten by the high pressure, so we've got to be clever about what we do. What we want is to be going east to get down into the Southern Ocean as fast as possible. It looks like we'll have to go upwind to get a change in the wind direction, which is absolutely what we don't want to do, but, looking at the scale of things, I think it's probably the safest option we have . . .

Francis had a great time down here: you just have to look at his averages of 16, 17 and 18 knots on the way down into the Southern Ocean. He had it pretty

good and didn't seem to have any major slow-ups on the way down. Let's just hope that we don't slow down too much. Our conditions are worse than the ones Francis had, and we're just going to have to do the best we can with them. We know we're going to have a rough time – I've talked about it with Commanders a lot, we've said that it's going to be hard, whatever happens it's going to be hard.

It's still very hard to rest when it's so hot and airless, even in the cuddy – you sleep for half an hour and then wake up with a sore throat. It's not very nice on board at the moment, it's just so hot, it's horrible. And because we're reaching there's a lot of spray about, which means that the whole cockpit is just encrusted with salt. Every time you go out you get soaked, so you too get covered in salt! It's pretty miserable conditions; it was much nicer going downwind in the Trades, as we did on the way to the Equator. Whatever happens, the next month at least is going to be incredibly taxing – let's just hope that the conditions after the Cape of Good Hope are stable enough to let me get a little bit of sleep at some stage.

DAY TWELVE 9/12/04
13 hours 58 minutes ahead
445 miles south-east of Salvador

We're still heading south in the South Atlantic, approaching the Trindade group of islands. It's getting a little bit less hot, which is fantastic; at 16 degrees south, so it's not quite as tropical as it was a few days ago. We'll be heading even further down into the Southern Ocean over the next couple of days. Right now there are quite a few depressions down there, and there is a big high sitting east of Cape Horn, which could cause us a lot of problems. The weather isn't that easy, but it's worth playing for, because once we get those westerlies things will be a lot better.

We're about to face some difficult and challenging conditions. The high pressure that we would normally have here in the South Atlantic has basically split into two, and to avoid being eaten by the second part of it we're going to have to sail due south, which means plunging deep into the Southern Ocean earlier than we would like. In about three days' time we're going to be in freezing conditions, sailing under the Tristan da Cunha Islands and heading east in the westerlies. It's not ideal, but it's what we've got.

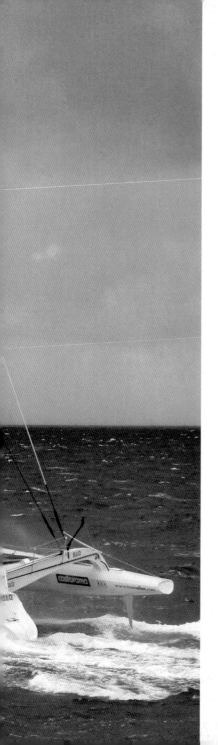

We'll have to plunge south pretty soon – we'll be at 40 degrees south before we know it, and it's not the best zone for icebergs. It's a bit worrying, to be quite honest

were up and down a bit, and I'm worried about what will happen in the south, because we're going to have an absolute shocker. You know the closer you get, the more you realize it's going to be pretty horrible. We'll have to plunge south pretty soon – we'll be at 40 degrees south before we know it, and it's not the best zone for icebergs. It's a bit worrying, to be quite honest. Conditions have been up and down in the last two hours: we've had the wind direction switching from 66 degrees to 100 – it's all over the place.

We're thirteen hours ahead of Francis at the moment, but there's no doubt we're going to lose time on him soon, because when he plunged into the Southern Ocean he was going south-east, which is a more direct route. But I'm not too worried about losing time on the record. When you do this kind of trip, it's swings and roundabouts. We'll have good times and bad times; and there is obviously a very bad time ahead of us, so we're likely to lose all we've gained on Francis. But, hopefully, there will be times when we will gain and then won't lose that. That's the way it works out here – you've just got to do your best, keep trucking on and get the best out of the weather that you've got. That's what I'm concentrating on, trying to focus on the big picture.

DAY THIRTEEN 10/12/04
13 hours 53 minutes ahead
720 miles east of Rio

**We're nearly at the 5,000-mile mark –
sometimes it feels like the trip
has already taken a month, and
at others like we just left
yesterday.** It's an extraordinary feeling –
it's a bit like time stops on board. You
have your routines, you're managing the
little world around you, and you've got to
concentrate hard on doing that as best
as you possibly can.

It looks like we're going to be keeping
more breeze for the next 24–36 hours than
we thought, which is great news. We'll be
able to keep pushing the boat, maintaining
good speed, for quite a while longer, but it
all depends how this little low underneath
us evolves and how quickly the high
behind us moves. We've basically got to,
at some point, get into the low-pressure
systems of the south. We have to make
that change, that transition. The big
question is: when will that happen and

how painful will it be?

When we actually do get into the strong winds of the low-pressure systems, we're looking at maybe 35–40 knots of breeze. The sea is going to be very confused, and we'll just have to turn into the waves – it's going to be very, very uncomfortable and horrible for the boat. We'll need to throttle back and take it easy as we try not to break anything. Once we get into the wind from the north and the north-west in the right direction, we can 'pump up the volume' when the waves will allow us, and go a bit faster.

The boat's been absolutely fantastic. I couldn't wish for better. She's performed brilliantly. She sails fantastically; she's a pleasure to sail. Sailing her is physical, and very hard, but I don't think I could have a better boat for the job – if anything is letting us down, it's me! Working her to her potential for twenty-four hours a day is incredibly taxing. I'm doing my best and pushing her as hard as I feel that I can. I'm trying to get as much rest as possible, whenever possible, but it's very, very tough. At the end of the day, I'm the engine that drives the boat, so I'm the limiting factor. I'm just trying to give as much as I absolutely can to get the best speeds out of her while looking after her as well.

DAY FOURTEEN 11/12/04
1 day 2 hours 11 minutes ahead
940 miles north-east of Tristan da Cunha

We've passed the 5,000-mile mark and we're a day ahead of Francis. It's good to be ahead, there's no doubt about it. I'd rather be ahead than behind, but at the same time we know it's early days. We've only been out here two weeks – we've got another eight at least to go, so anything can change in that time. Although it's good to be ahead and that's a positive, you can't count your chickens until they're hatched and they're certainly far from being hatched right now.

The South Atlantic didn't look great to start with, but so far it's turned out to be pretty good. We're a third of the way from Brazil and two thirds of the way from South Africa, so we've been doing OK, but we're still a long way from being in the south. Things will get a lot more stressful over the next forty-eight hours. Right now we're in a nice, warm climate – it's still pretty warm on board, and we've got sunshine. But we'll be diving south soon, where it'll be freezing cold and we'll be sitting in front of a fairly potent Southern Ocean depression system. How I feel right now, I'd love to get into the

cold weather, but give it a couple of days and I'm sure I'll be pretty keen to get somewhere warm again! It really is brutally cold down there. It'll be freezing – water temperature down to 2–3 degrees – and life on board can be pretty miserable, so it's going to be a big change. And it'll happen very, very quickly, so I'm just preparing myself for that as best as I possibly can.

I'm concerned about the rudders as we go into the Southern Ocean because we'll get absolutely hammered down there. We'll see worse than the worst we saw in the

North Atlantic, when we were going fast and reaching and getting hit by waves, which is what caused the fuse problem in the first place. It's likely this could get worse and become a bigger issue. You walk round the boat and you see things getting tired and you change lashings and you worry about whether the autopilot rams are getting tired but, at the end of the day, with a boat averaging such high speeds, you'll have problems. You're not wondering *if* something will break. You're wondering *what* will break.

I've had my head thrown against the roof of the boat and my feet thrown against the floor on numerous occasions. I was even airborne about six times during the night

DAY FIFTEEN 12/12/04
21 hours 23 minutes ahead
2,030 miles north-east of the
Cape of Good Hope

We are sitting in a weather front in the South Atlantic, and we've been in here now since the early hours of the morning. We've seen a maximum of 37 knots of wind, but the biggest enemy is actually the sea, because the waves are absolutely huge and in this breeze we're just flying off them and then crashing back down. The noise the boat is making is horrendous, as are the noises I'm making as I bounce off the sides of the boat. I've had no sleep at all. The sea conditions are terrible. I hope I'm not in these conditions again on the trip. Doing anything is virtually impossible. I've been trying to do some things this morning, and it's even difficult just to move inside the boat – you're permanently holding on to something, you're permanently getting thrown around. I've, literally, been thrown

off the chart table seat; I've had my head thrown against the roof of the boat and my feet thrown against the floor on numerous occasions. I was even airborne about six times during the night. The boat is standing up to it amazingly, and I'm trying to hang in there as well.

We've had a number of technical issues since the beginning of the trip, and the charging has been preying on my mind the most. After a week of being at sea, I realized the main generating engine was using a massive amount of oil and that that amount of oil was not sustainable – in other words, I didn't have enough oil to complete the trip with that engine. So, after going through a whole process of different tests, I've now switched from the main generating engine to the small generator – which has brought an entire

host of other problems, like ventilating the boat and trying to keep the temperature down in the cabin. The smaller generator is 'air-cooled', rather than 'water-cooled', which means that it gets very hot, as it is sucking air from the cabin and pushing it out even hotter! The temperature in the main generating room went up to 48 degrees the first time I ran it, and that was with all the hatches open. It's also incredibly noisy and creates only a maximum of 55 amps from its alternator, whereas the other one is about 200 amps. So it means lots and lots of charging with the engine running for longer periods of time. It's been hugely stressful, and it's still preying on my mind – we've not used it enough yet to know for sure whether it can do the job for the rest of the voyage, or whether I can deal with the fumes.

Before we left, we did look at the back-up plans that we could put into practice on board if it became necessary. Since the boat was built, we've always had the back-up generator in. It's not there to completely replace what the main generator does, but it is there to tide us over, and that's exactly what it's doing. But to have this problem and to be using the back-up generator after just two weeks at sea is a bit of a knock. At the same time there's still a glimmer of hope that for the last few weeks, once I get round Cape Horn, I may be able to run the main generator on a different kind of oil, and things on board could improve again.

I've also had problems with one of the water-makers, which has given up on me. Yesterday I tried to run it with the generator and there was a strange noise coming from it, so I stopped it. Today I tried to run it without the generator, which involves using more of the boat's power, but that didn't work either.

It's been pretty demoralizing – every time we seem to solve a problem to some extent, another one comes along, or something else stops working

The situation is serious, but you just have to hope that everything continues working and that it's going to keep working like that for the next month or so to get you round. From a personal point of view, it's been unbelievably stressful coping with these problems and sailing the boat in these conditions. Today I've been trying to sort out ventilation for the generator, trying to attach fans to hatches, trying to wire things up, and getting thrown round the boat as I've been going along. I tried to rewire the heater I have by the generator and use it purely as a fan, just to move the hot air away from the engine. Fumbling around under the floor, trying to rewire ten wires coming in from all different cable runs, was not very pleasurable. Bushed and sweaty, scrabbling in the diesel oil that had spilled from the heater fuel pipe ... This, together with doing the equivalent of an oil change when the boat's powering up and falling over waves of up to 30–40 feet high ... Not exactly my idea of fun ... So it's been pretty demoralizing – every time we seem to solve a problem to some extent, another one comes along, or something else stops working. It's been a very, very difficult first couple of weeks, and it's not really ideal to be going into the Southern Ocean tired and exhausted from the problems we've already had.

DAY SIXTEEN 13/12/04
9 hours 56 minutes ahead
1,825 miles west of the Cape of Good Hope

I got some sleep this morning and some this afternoon, but I need more, I need a lot more. I'm absolutely fried; last night was the pits, and I nearly had to pull out. It was that close. I'd got to the stage where I couldn't breathe in the boat, I couldn't charge the batteries, I couldn't make any water. I was absolutely at my wits' end. But I've managed to improve the situation with the generator by setting up a ducting system, which means I've got cooler air coming in now, and the temperature is not rising so fast. This has enabled me, I think, to block off the airflows and to reduce the fumes within the living area. We'll have to see how this holds up on the next full charge this morning, but it's a step forward.

It's still up to 43 degrees, but at least there're no fumes in the boat. The heat

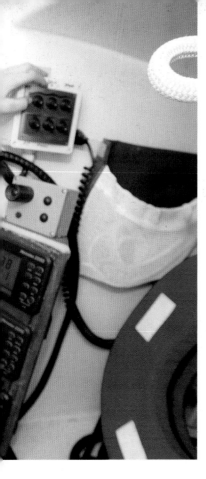

daggerboard, then using a hose I pinched from the portable bilge pump to pull water up from it to the water-maker via the tank breather. *B&Q* has effectively 'two storeys' to her hulls, and in the main hull I can virtually stand up on both levels. Trying to strap the pipe to the bottom of the ballast tank was not much fun, with a ton of water surging around in the bottom of the tank trying to knock me over and seriously soaking me. Eventually I got it working and at least now I have a few litres of fresh water. I'm exhausted, but I'm going to try to fix the other one too. I've also got another problem: the batteries are going down much faster than they were, but I don't know what exactly is wrong. We're taking 10 amps, and I can't find where the power is going. I last finished a charge less than six hours ago and I already need to charge again, so I'm a little bit concerned. I'm supposed to charge every eight hours, not every six, and there's a huge difference between eight and six hours in fuel consumption.

I tried to sleep for an hour or two in my bag, but it was fitful, too hot, too cold, with too many worries going around in my head. But I know I need to sleep more. It's been a real mission – this has taken me to my complete end, but I'm still hanging in there. Let's just hope the hard part is now over and it's going to get a little bit easier. I need some time to recover. From a technical point of view I think we've managed to sustain our position particularly well, despite the many problems that we've had. The issue is just the reliability of the charging systems that we have, how we're going to use these systems in the future, and whether they're going to survive until the end of the trip.

should decrease once I get down south. I'll be sucking in cooler air, which should help enormously with the engine. I feel really trashed and unsettled by all this. It's going to take a while for the pain to go away. I screamed out loud when I started the generator and the new ventilation system worked. I have a load of DIY to do before it's finished properly, but the principle works.

I've also fixed the second water-maker, so we have one running again. Took me hours to work it out: the problem was with the water-intake system, but I couldn't see why it was happening. I ended up filling the emergency ballast around the

DAY SEVENTEEN 14/12/04
4 hours 2 minutes ahead
Passes Tristan da Cunha

The motto for today is SLEEP MORE – SUFFER LESS. I tried to engrave this on my brain last night, tried with all my energy to sleep – easier said than done sometimes – but, hey, we have to try ... Just as it went dark I called into the weather routers and said, 'I'll be sailing for the next few hours under solent and full main, I don't care what the wind does, or where the wind takes me – I'll call you in 3 hours,' and I did. I stripped off, jumped into a warm sleeping bag in my bunk for the first time, and, though just for 2 hours, I slept. Conditions were thankfully quite calm last night, as we were sailing towards a high-pressure system.

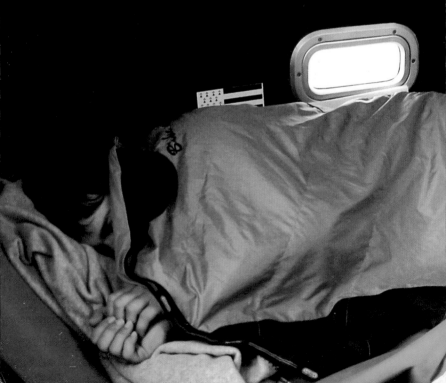

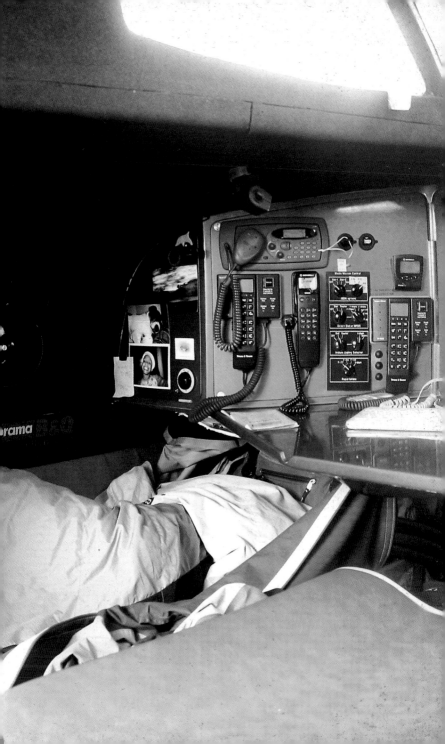

The trials and tribulations of the last few days seem miles away. Things are under control

After the horrors of the previous 36 hours — upwind in over 30 knots and a mountainous sea — everything now seems almost surreal. This morning I awoke from my beanbag (you see the bunk couldn't last that long!) to 4 beautiful albatrosses circling behind *B&Q*. The first I've seen on this trip, and as beautiful and magnificent as ever. Not only that, but for the first time I find myself feeling a bit more at home on *B&Q*. This morning after the albatrosses I couldn't sleep, so I did some sorting, found places to stow things that had previously been badly stowed in bags, put up a few pictures in the cabin that had been stored away in a box. You know, almost homely things. On top of all this, the wind has filled in, and we have a relatively flat sea. We're charging ahead with genoa and full main, and on our starboard side I can see the beautiful island of Tristan da Cunha ... The sky is grey, but I like that ... I almost prefer it to the beating sun of the Equator. But that will all change soon, I'm sure. This morning Ellen has found herself again ... not only that, but she has rediscovered the magic of being out here. The trials and tribulations of the last few days seem miles away. Things are under control, and we're heading SOUTH!!

ellen xx

The difference in my outlook between now and forty-eight hours ago is absolutely black and white. We've had some terrible problems, and it really did seem like the odds were stacked against us for a long period of time. The boat seems back on track now. The charge seems under control, there have been a few issues with it, but nothing too bad, and it's actually possible to be inside the boat and charging the batteries at the same time now. Things are much, much better, my outlook is much, much more positive, and I'm sure that a little bit of hot air will not do any harm, in the Southern Ocean anyway. Sailing past the island of Tristan da Cunha and seeing the albatrosses has certainly changed the vista and, to some extent, my outlook this morning!

MORE !
LESS :

USHA
EOUA
GOOD
LEEW
H
EOUA
USHAN

WE'RE THROUGH

YA. HOO !

DIG
DEEP

BELIEVE

+VC

DAY EIGHTEEN 15/12/04
14 hours 29 minutes ahead
1,085 miles south-west of the
Cape of Good Hope

We've had some fast 24-hour runs.

At the moment we're tending to slow the boat rather than speed it up, because the sea conditions are getting worse, the daily runs are going to be slower rather than faster. Things have been fantastic: we've had good breeze overnight, good waves, good wind conditions, and the boat was sailing quickly. It's been really good to be able to push her in the relatively flat seas that we had yesterday evening and to be able to feel her sliding very, very easily and nicely through the waves.

We're trying to make a course of due east rather than dropping into the south, because at the moment the breeze is basically from the north-west, which makes it very difficult for us to sail the ideal course. But that breeze is going to drop back into the west, and then we'll gybe over and head south-east. If we go too far south with this northerly breeze, then when we get the westerly breeze, we're going to end up too far south on it and too close to the ice. So we're sailing an easterly course at the moment as fast as possible. We're further south than Francis was last year, and we're gaining on him all the time just because we're further south and so, effectively, sailing a shorter course. We're currently about fifteen hours ahead of him, and we don't seem to have any huge light patches of wind – maybe a few hours tonight – so on the whole we should be able to keep up a pretty reasonable speed between here and the Cape of Good Hope.

Things are getting a little bit chilly now, and the water temperature has dropped down to about 15 degrees. The sky is a vast greyness, and the sun has disappeared – we're in our first Southern Ocean depression. We're actually at 38 22´s – almost officially in the Southern Ocean. You're generally in when you're under 40 degrees south, so it definitely feels like the Southern Ocean. We'll be down here for a long time, so from here on things change both mentally and physically.

DAY NINETEEN 16/12/04
13 hours 57 minutes ahead
660 miles south-west of the
Cape of Good Hope

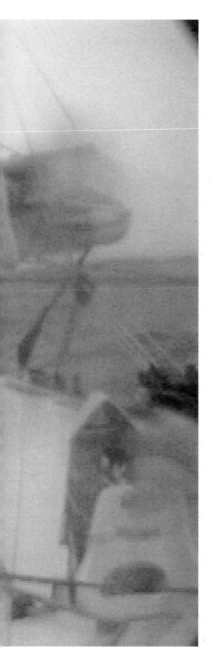

A few thoughts for a very wet morning while we await the passing of a rainy front. I look out of *B&Q*'s windows and see big grey waves and monotonous drizzle. Our world has closed in around us, and we can see very, very little other than the 400-metre radius. We have more wind than I thought we'd see right now — quite gusty, but averaging around 25 to 28 knots. But we're sailing along OK — and with the changeable conditions I'm sure that we're doing the right thing by not pushing too hard . . . We should be gybing in a few hours anyway — so pulling out the third reef would not be the right thing now.

I was thinking in the early hours of this morning about life on board, and about the differences between what we have here and what we experience on land. I think the first thing is that this little world of *B&Q* and me feels like a small island. We hope that we shall have all we need, but know that we can improvise for what we have not. There is only so much of everything, so each square of kitchen roll, each centimetre of tape used, gets you closer to having none left. Everything is checked before it goes in the bin just to be sure it's not wanted. You need to be resourceful and to tackle problems rationally and simply as they arise. There will always be problems, always ... You just hope that they'll be surmountable and dealable with — the rest is a logical waiting game. In reality, it's quite a simple life.

I think that it's healthy to put other things before you sometimes, like putting the boat first — if I let

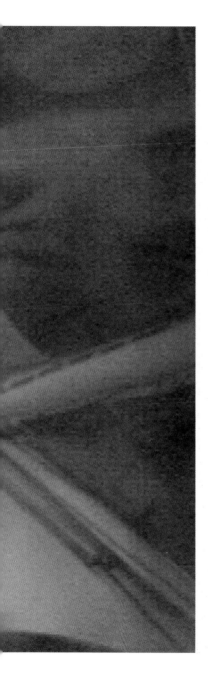

her state slide, then I know she'll
be less able to look after me too.

I am very aware of the level of
her batteries; each drop of fuel for
charging is measured. Lights are
never left on unnecessarily; the kettle
is always filled with 15 pumps of the
tap – just enough for a freeze-dried
meal and a cup of tea. Not more, not
less. It's about managing this little
space, keeping it as dry and as warm
as I can. I don't have much here,
really, there are no luxuries – just a
few CDs and the odd photo scattered
around. But I'm so lucky because the
pleasure is inside me, the luxuries
are inside me. Those moments shared
with friends and loved ones, the
simple things that make people smile
– they're with me all the time. They're
priceless and, luckily for my
endeavour, weightless too!

It's funny the way your mind
works when you're sitting on a boat,
in the middle of a huge grey expanse
of beautiful ocean . . .

That's it for now . . .

ellen

**I look out of *B&Q*'s
windows and see
big grey waves and
monotonous drizzle.
Our world has closed
in around us**

Weather reports showed the wind decreasing, but we still seem to have 20–25 knots, which just proves that the weather files for the Southern Ocean are fairly unreliable and that you can never really trust them. At about midnight last night, I was speaking to Commanders: the breeze had gone down to 20 knots and they said, 'Yeah, that's it, the wind's backing off now, it's going to decrease and rotate.' But it hasn't. It's basically sat in front of us and hasn't decreased, hasn't rotated, and it's in pretty much the same direction now that it's been in for the past few days.

I changed the sails because we thought the breeze was going to decrease. I took the staysail down and I took out the third reef, which is quite a manoeuvre in itself, and then the breeze started to rise again. Since then I've stayed with the same sail configuration, and with this amount of breeze we're pretty much OK. But if it increases any more than this, I'm going to have to change sails again quite soon.

On the whole I feel different, and am much better than I have been over the last few weeks. I feel more positive. I feel more comfortable in the Southern Ocean than I did at the Equator when it was so hot. It's a shame I'll not be able to get that heater on as we go further south. It's already really

cold at night. You get all sweaty from sail changes and then freeze when you try to sleep in your damp oilskins. Even when you can take the oilskins off and get into your bunk, it takes you ages to warm up again because you've got so cold.

I don't think anyone should go to the Southern Ocean without having some fear of it. It's a very, very desolate place. You're at the end of the earth, in the middle of nowhere, no one really lives here, there are just a few scattered islands down in the freezing water. It's an amazing place to sail. I'm about to go round the bottom of the earth, quite a strange concept to come to terms with. It's exciting – but at the same time very dangerous.

I don't think anyone should go to the Southern Ocean without having some fear of it. It's a very, very desolate place. You're at the end of the earth, in the middle of nowhere

DAY TWENTY 17/12/04
16 hours 16 minutes ahead
Fastest solo time to the Cape of Good Hope

We had a horrible night; I've had hardly any sleep. We had a really changeable breeze, and everything was up and down, but we seem to have come out of it OK. We've got reasonable boat speed this morning and a good breeze. I'm sailing along with blue skies, which makes a huge difference after what we were sailing in. There are quite a few petrels and albatrosses around.

We opened our second bottle of champagne as we passed by South Africa and the Cape of Good Hope. We're now officially, 100 per cent, three hulls and the skipper, in the Southern Ocean! Let's go! It's fantastic that we've managed to beat Francis's time – it's certainly a positive for our debut in the Southern Ocean.

The Cape of Good Hope marks the boundary between the South Atlantic and the Indian Ocean. In a few hours' time we'll be leaving the South Atlantic, and we won't be back until we round Cape Horn

heading north. The Indian Ocean is renowned for its bad storms and its depressions, which track down from Africa. They tend to be very energetic depressions with strong winds and can sometimes build very, very quickly. That can lead to a very dangerous situation. These storms can suddenly pull south and become very aggressive. You have to be extra vigilant, watching every satellite picture, to try to stay *in* the best winds and *out* of the particularly venomous areas that could end the attempt.

I managed to get some sleep – I put on the generator and the 'high-wind' alarm and got into my bunk. I tried to sleep, but I had to get up to do a sail change – that happened three times today. Sleeping in the cuddy is not ideal: did that once in the night after a sail change when I got pretty sweaty, then dragged my blanket over me. Woke up absolutely freezing and it's not even that cold yet!

DAY TWENTY-ONE 18/12/04
20 hours 17 minutes ahead
205 miles east of the Cape of Good Hope

Though we've had a few more-than-scary moments over the last 24 hours down here, there have also been some incredible ones too. We're in a huge Southern Ocean swell – a mountainous seascape, hard to imagine, within which the huge waves roll away as far as the eye can see . . .

Last night was a dark night, hard to see anything out there – nothing but the constant noise of *B&Q* speeding through the water, the howling wind and the breaking of the waves. The waves are so steep here that poor *B&Q* feels like she's either running down a hill or being pushed hard up one. Waves regularly break

We're in a huge Southern Ocean swell – a mountainous seascape, hard to imagine, within which the huge waves roll away as far as the eye can see

mountain, how fast, how far and when will we hit the bottom . . .

Last night I did a series of sail changes which had the adrenalin pumping hard – wind speeds were up above 45 knots, and our surfs were regularly over 30 knots. (And all this while plummeting down unpredictable slopes of black powerful sea in the dark . . .)

Sunrise, though, was amazing – the light fantastic, and the seabirds, as ever, around us all the time. Wandering albatrosses, sooty albatrosses, black-bellied storm petrels, and little shearwaters – dancing not just in the wind but with the immense waves. I guess for them it's just another day in the Southern Ocean. As for me, sometimes I find it hard to come to terms with the idea that this is in fact my job.

ellen xx

on the windward float quarter. What is noticeable through the dark, shining brighter than our glowing instruments, are the crests of phosphorescence – unbelievable, beautiful – and at times immense. We spend our time, even when trying to rest huddled in a ball in the cuddy, just feeling where we are on each

Last night was pretty stressful – it certainly had its moments. The breeze went up to 46 knots as I was doing a fairly delicate sail change with a 'boat speed' in excess of 30 knots – I had to work so hard to get the sails changed that the back of my throat felt like it was going to drop out, it was burning.

The sea is unbelievable. It's like sailing over mountains. It's like driving an all-terrain vehicle very fast over mountains. Sometimes you're coasting down the hills and other times you're fighting up the hills, except that the mountains are moving – you're always sliding along with the mountains. It's absolutely spectacular and the seas really are big. We went over a seamount where the depth went from 4,000 m to 1,000 m and the sea state was horrible – we got 3 knots of counter-current! I thought there was something wrong with the speedo and kept thinking this is crazy, and then I saw the seamount on the chart and realized. It went on for ages afterwards. The breeze is beginning to die off now, which is flattening things out a little bit, but in the early hours of this morning when the sun rose it was magnificent. We've done a few dangerous surfs while going very, very quickly, but I have to say the boat's been just awesome, she's handling it really well. The views, the waves, the breaking water,

the albatrosses and the wildlife are just spectacular, particularly yesterday evening as the sun set.

I'm concerned about the ice, which is always a worry, and if we keep sailing along in this direction for the next twenty-four hours there is no doubt that we'll see some ice. Hopefully we'll be able to gybe before we get down to the 5-degree mark.

We'll just have to monitor that over the next few hours.

We've begun to slow down now, and shortly we're going to gybe and head to the east. The sea conditions are quite big and the wind conditions are fairly light, so that's going to make the boat's speeds very slow. Although there's a new weather system coming in from the west and we stand to make some good miles, the sea conditions are actually very rough and trying to go fast in these conditions is not going to be easy. It's stupid to try to push the boat harder, because all it takes is a strong gust, too much sail, then we could flip and it would all be over. Might change to solent if it gets lighter, then wait to gybe. Full on!!!

DAY TWENTY-TWO 19/12/04
1 day 4 hours 21 minutes ahead
240 miles north of the Prince Edward Islands

It's a very special day today because it's Mobi's first birthday. *B&Q* went into the water exactly one year ago in Sydney, and she's done 30,000 miles of sailing since then. We had a little celebration for her this morning. I opened the small bottle of champagne I had reserved for Christmas, as I thought this was a better day to celebrate. I did a little colouring and made a rosette for the boat saying 1 today. On the whole spirits are quite good, although it's been a bit disappointing this morning to have less wind than was forecast.

The last twenty-four hours have given over to the approach of a low-weather system from the west. We've had a good night of sailing with good speeds. We were at over 20 knots for a lot of it, and we touched at over twenty-four hours ahead of the record – that felt good. Sadly this morning the weather's been playing up – it's been very changeable. The breeze has

been down to 15 knots then up to 25. I'm hoping it's going to increase once more – it should be blowing 25–30 knots, maybe even with gusts of 40. Right now, we've got a lot less wind than that, so fingers crossed it will return.

We're currently north-west of Marion Island, about 250 miles north of the Antarctic Convergence Line and heading just north of east. The seas are a lot flatter than they have been, but they are due to build again towards this evening, with stronger winds tomorrow. It is going to get fairly hairy again fairly soon, so now is a good time to rest. Did manage to get into my bunk on three occasions last night, which was quite special.

One of the hardest things is sailing at night when there's no moon – the waves are 30–40 feet and you can't see what's ahead of you. You do have to have a lot of faith in the boat, and you've got to have faith in yourself – that you're going to

make the right decisions, like changing sails at the right time. And not over-powering the boat – you might wipe out at the bottom of a wave, and obviously the consequences of wiping out are fairly serious. Just trying to drive the boat hard and maintain high averages when you're flying down a wave and can't see where you're going is pretty difficult!

I try very hard not to think of the targets on the course, because we don't have the same weather that Francis had; we just aren't going to have the same weather. There will be times when we have better weather, and there will be times when we have worse weather. It's the only way to view it. If you give as much as you can as soon as you can, then you'll be OK, but

setting yourself goals is dangerous because the pressure's already very great out here. At the moment we're ahead of Francis by over twenty-four hours after three weeks, and it's good to have a lead on him. But the weather situation ahead doesn't look fantastic, with a light area of winds coming up which we're going to have to try to negotiate around. If we lose a few hours it wouldn't surprise me at all. I'm also really worried about a big depression forming on our track that I don't think we'll be able to avoid. It's still six days away, just east of Kerguelen, but at the moment I don't know how we're going to avoid it. We have to avoid the 50–60 knot winds at all costs, even if we actually have to stop.

I think I must be the luckiest person in the world to be here, seeing, feeling, smelling and touching all this with my own eyes and senses – I feel alive

DAY TWENTY-THREE 20/12/04
18 hours 4 minutes ahead
400 miles west of the Crozet Islands

It's about to go dark down here, and the waves are no smaller . . . In fact, now we've gybed they seem bigger and more powerful than before. I'm completely in awe of this place. The beauty of those immense rolling waves is endless, and there is a kind of eternal feeling about their majestic rolling that will live on for ever. Watching them roll along – with nothing to stop them – makes me and B&Q feel completely insignificant. They're hardly aware of our tiny presence on their surface. The birds are numerous and varied, and they seem cheekier today – getting closer and playing with the wind on our forestay. I stand in the cockpit and stare – I think I must be the luckiest person in the world to be here, seeing, feeling, smelling and touching all this with my own eyes and senses – I feel alive. But it's still quite frightening being here and feeling poor B&Q being hurled down the waves as she was earlier – winds gusting not to 40 but to over 50–55 knots in the squalls. Now that the sun is setting there will be no visual way of knowing where we are on the waves, just that constant knot in my stomach wondering what will happen at the foot of the wave before us. There is some kind of mesmerizing feeling, some kind of completeness, about being here. I feel this is not so far from the end of the earth; we are isolated, isolated, but, on the other hand, completely free. I'm glad we've come down here and seen this storm. It's a reminder of how small and insignificant we are on this planet – but at the same time what a responsibility we have towards its protection . . .

DAY TWENTY-FOUR 21/12/04
20 hours 34 minutes ahead
53 miles west of the Crozet Islands

We were in some pretty big seas today. In many ways we were forced south because of certain seamounts, which meant that we couldn't really gybe because the sea conditions were far too dangerous. I was pushed to the south, and 50–55 knots of breeze were the most we saw, with a sustained 40 knots for a long period of time. It was pretty hairy, but I have to say that the boat was absolutely incredible. To have been surfing at 25–28 knots in that amount of breeze in those waves, to have handled it as well as she did – I was just absolutely over the moon

with her performance. It was fantastic.

Right now, things have changed enormously: we've got a much flatter sea and we've got loads and loads of wildlife with us. We're just to the north of the Crozet Islands. I couldn't see them, although I was only forty-four miles away. When you have all of the birds from the islands around, you feel you're closer to land, you can see kelp in the water and a bit of life, so it's been a good morning. The last thirty-six hours, even in the storm, were just mind blowing! To be in such huge seas and to see the power of nature

– to be on an ocean that isn't flat in any way but more like a mountain range! There is no horizon because the sea is going up and down so much. It was an incredible experience and one I wouldn't change for the world, despite the fact that it was very windy and slightly frightening at times – it was simply unbelievable.

There is a storm coming which will hit us on Christmas Day. The weather models today make it seem a little bit smaller than it was yesterday, so it'll have a little bit less breeze. But we're talking about a consistent 50 knots, which will be pretty hard to escape. Once you get into winds of 40 knots, 50 knots and touching on 60 it becomes a battle to slow the boat down – and to keep her 'tamed' in a cauldron of sea. You've got the wing mast, which is 45 square metres of surface in itself, like a sail pushing you along, and that you can't take down. You have to think about all of these things in advance; you've got to be really practical. If we do need to climb to the north to get round this depression, which looks likely,

then we may be doing that over the next couple of days. But we're watching it very closely to see how it evolves. It's going to be quite hard going, so I don't think it's going to be a particularly relaxing Christmas, whatever happens!

I've had a couple of technical issues this morning which I've been working on. I discovered a problem with the steering system yesterday night, though it's not major. The bottom bearing of the laystock for the main rudder was moving a little bit and some of the screws had undone themselves. So I've made some small carbon wedges this morning and wedged them all the way round and taped them up there. It looks like it should be OK. The second issue is that I've been back down with the main rudder today. We've had some more movement there, so I've tightened up the fuses for the kick-up system and also taped some more wedges in the back. So it's been all go this morning, lots of practical work trying to make sure the boat is OK for the next stage.

I've discovered a new problem: I've gone off muesli bars and, unfortunately, I based my diet on eating loads of them!

DAY TWENTY-FIVE 22/12/04
20 hours 14 minutes ahead
445 miles WNW of the Kerguelen Islands

Water temperature was down to 5 degrees the other day, which always opens your eyes a little and makes you wonder what's around.

There is definitely a big ice risk coming up. There are icebergs further north, amongst the islands off New Zealand, than they would usually be, so I think we're going to have to end up going underneath them. It's going to be pretty stressful down there; we're going to have to be very, very vigilant.

The sea temperature is up to over 10 degrees today and we've got a bit of

sunshine, which is nice, keeps everything a bit warmer. We had 30 knots this morning, but right now we're sailing in 22–23 knots, making it just about time to pull that extra reef out. Things are good; the boat's in good form.

We're going to pass the Kerguelen Islands, which is always special. I was a bit upset not to see the Crozet Islands yesterday, and it doesn't look like I'm going to get to see the Kerguelen Islands either. But you're still aware of them, as a lot more birds and wildlife are about. It's great to be down here and feeling those

islands around us. But there is also a small tinge of sadness when I remember the *Jules Verne*: it was just two years ago that we lost our mast down here. I'm very conscious of that and it concerns me, obviously.

I'm also very aware that there is no way for us to avoid the Christmas storm. Going north is not going to keep us out of it. It is going to hit us; we can't get away from this one. All we can do is try to move as far to the east as fast as we possibly can, to try to stay in front of it. Whatever happens it's going to be

horrible. It'll be very windy and just survival conditions for a short period of time. So I'm just going to do my best, sail as fast as I can and hope that we can stay ahead of that front for several days to come.

I've discovered a new problem: I've gone off muesli bars and, unfortunately, I based my diet on eating loads of them! Worse, I've gone off porridge as well. On top of that my calorie intake did depend a lot on the olive oil, which of course we're saving for the generator. So all in all the diet is not as good as it needs to be!

DAY TWENTY-SIX 23/12/04
15 hours 57 minutes ahead
270 miles north of the Kerguelen Islands

I'm a bit shaken up after the collision last night – I was on the phone talking to Loïk, the Boat Captain, about the water-maker when I got thrown forward on to the chart table. I rushed outside and checked all the rudders, checked underneath at the daggerboard, and there didn't seem to be any damage. But we stopped pretty suddenly. We were sailing at 26 knots when we slowed to 20, which was obviously quite abrupt, but I'm glad there doesn't seem to be any damage – let's just hope nothing appears in the future. It was more of a shock knowing that we had hit something, but the boat seems OK. I was very, very lucky, I think.

I've been bailing water out of the float today and checking things over before this storm, making sure all the hatches are sealed and just going over the boat. I've got to be sure we're OK because we're going to get our arses kicked for the next three or four days. It's about breaking down the preparation into manageable chunks. Mentally, it's important to feel ready. It's important to try to manage stress by making sure you're ready to change the right sail, that all the sheets are led in the right place and nothing's going to chafe.

Christmas is a big question mark right now, because it's either going to be a day when we stay ahead of the front and sail to the east very fast, or when we get caught up by the front and end up in a 50-knot breeze with very little behind it and very rough seas. To be in big 50-knot seas in a boat that is 75 feet long is an experience in itself. Although *B&Q* is a big boat, she seems absolutely minuscule in those waves – they're breaking underneath us, they're breaking over us, we're surfing down them – and we just appear completely and utterly insignificant within them. Sailing down a mountain-sized wave at 28, 29, 30 knots on a surf, your heart is absolutely in your mouth and every time you wonder what is going to happen at the bottom of this wave. Will her bows pull back up again? Will we simply cartwheel into the next wave's face?

There is very little time even to think about the fact that it's going to be Christmas and that I'll be missing my family. So perhaps concentrating on the boat and the tactics is the best thing. For me, out here, dates like Christmas aren't important. It's the dates that I've created that are driving me, like passing Cape Leeuwin or Cape Horn. They motivate me more than the fact that it's Christmas. But I will be thinking about my family celebrating Christmas together and that I won't be there, yet again, with them.

This clock is continuously counting down and its numbers are what dictate my life. The best Christmas present ever would be to arrive at the finish line before it reaches zero

DAY TWENTY-SEVEN 24/12/04

3 hours 37 minutes ahead
1,360 miles north-east of the
Kerguelen Islands

We're currently sailing along in relatively stable conditions, and the breeze is lighter than it has been for a while. It's nice and sunny at the moment, but this is literally the calm before the storm, as we're waiting for the storm that's going to hammer us on Christmas Day. In the next few hours the wind is due to increase, and a very powerful front will be passing over us during tonight and tomorrow. Things are going to get pretty hairy on board, so tomorrow is going to be a bit of a survival game: the main thing is to come out the other side with myself and the boat in one piece. But when you see a storm coming with such a powerful front it's pretty disconcerting. I'm trying to sleep as and when I can, be that inside or out – just trying to lie down and close my eyes. But there have already been several sail changes today, and it's proving to be quite

taxing, as the breeze is very unstable right now. Things might just steady out, though I doubt it very much. I think the next rest we're going to get will be in about three days' time.

We're only a third of the way round the world – all we can do is our best. I'm concentrating on getting through the next couple of days. Obviously you've got to have some confidence that you can make it round the world, but at the same time it's a very long way between here and the finish. It's far too early to say.

I'm trying to get some rest, trying to make sure the boat's ready – I've been checking her over, making sure there are no issues, nothing that's going to come up and bite us when the wind gets very, very strong – and basically just trying to prepare myself mentally for what's going to be a very difficult forty-eight hours.

DAY TWENTY-EIGHT
25/12/04, Christmas Day
10 hours 37 minutes ahead
1,250 miles to Cape Leeuwin

We're in the centre of the storm – the only thing white about this Christmas is the breaking waves all around us. The conditions are horrendous, the waves are huge, and the boat is getting physically thrown around. I'm sailing in and out of a pretty angry front, but it's actually going to slow in front of us and we'll end up sailing back into that same storm, even if we fall out of the back of it today. I've had virtually no sleep: there's a leak over my bunk, so that's soaked. I've been in my oilskins for twelve hours now and I'm just hoping that this front is going to go over without doing too much damage to the boat or to me.

It doesn't feel like a different day, and I don't feel much in the Christmas spirit. I wondered what I could do for Christmas and I decided to make myself a double dose of sports drink. That's about the level of Christmas spirit on board. I've not been

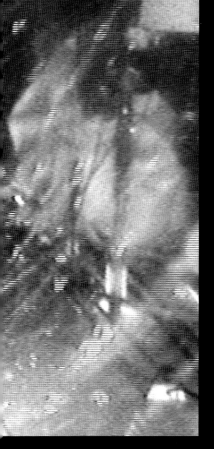

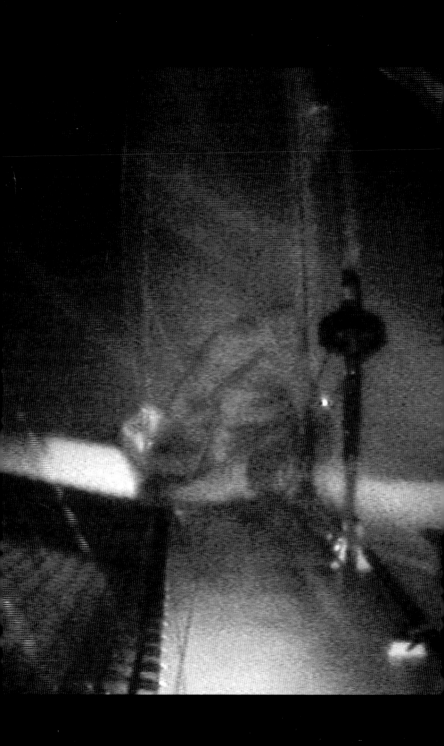

to find my Christmas bag at the back of the boat – it's too rough. I'm just trying to look after the boat and after myself, to keep everything turning until things get a little bit better. I'm hanging in there, I'm very tired, pretty cold now, spending a lot of time outside trimming the sails. It's been a pretty tiring Christmas so far, but I'm looking forward to seeing the light at the end of the tunnel in a few days.

There has been a lot of jolting, and earlier this morning we got taken by this one wave that literally just picked us up and threw us. The boat spun to starboard, landed almost dead down-wind and then spun 40–50 degrees. Everything went quiet as the wave broke over the back of us – then slewed us round so that we ended up pointing back up the wave. Before we accelerated

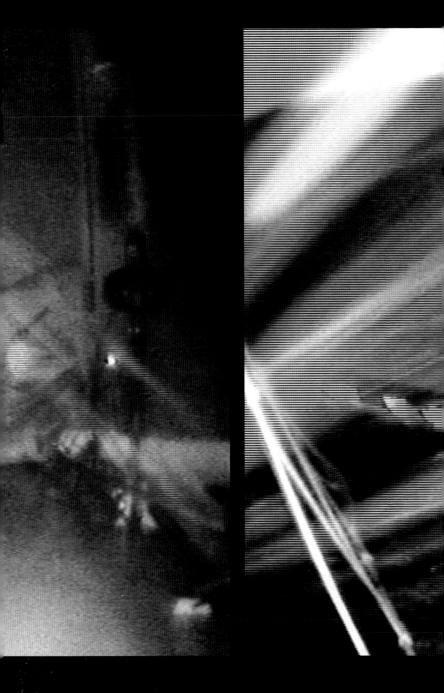

again we had another wave break right over the front of the boat – at a time when we were averaging 20–21 knots, so you can imagine what the inside of the boat was like. You have to keep your eyes on everything in these conditions. The charging's a nightmare; you can't even keep the diesel in the right place in the fuel tank. I had to restart the generator thirteen times during the last charge: it just kept dying. So *everything's* harder out here in this kind of weather.

We've just got to hang in there, really. We're in it now, it's hammering us, but we've got to try to deal with it as best we can. The boat is just unbelievable – she has taken so much hammering. And despite everything we've actually managed to gain on the record, which isn't a bad Christmas present!

DAY TWENTY-NINE 26/12/04
13 hours 47 minutes ahead
1,360 miles east of the Kerguelen Islands

Well, I'm a bit stuck for words this morning, in fact it's about 3 p.m. local time – that just about sums up my day, really. I have no idea how much sleep I've had, though I know it's not enough by far ... sleep is the rarest commodity out here, sleep and the time to eat. How many times have I said to myself: 'Shall I eat or sleep?' Basic but fundamental decisions. Yesterday was a day from hell, with horrendous conditions and a few 'full-on' moments when your heart is in your mouth – well, it's either that or your stomach, it all feels the same ... We physically got picked up by a freak wave yesterday, which made poor Mobi seem smaller than a duck in a swimming pool, that was probably the scariest moment of the trip so far – just not knowing where, or how we would land ... It's hardest when you have a few seconds to think about it. Normally when the waves hit you, it's bang, and the damage is done; when you're thrown, it's a much more prolonged fear, like waiting for

the trigger to be pulled – or not, as the case might be. We had two 'hits' yesterday: the first was being thrown, and the second was a solid wave landing on the boat as hard as if an elephant had been dropped on us from heaven. I thank my lucky stars that I was down below at the time, and that the damage was limited – but just to see the elastic parted like butter and the rope bags ripped off was humbling ... a statement of how irrelevant we are out here, and how we have to 'earn' our permit to pass ... It's not a place for bravado or complacency. This is real, very real, black and white real, and when you close your eyes that reality does not slip away. The odds are only magnified in your head, reminding you that there's no way out but to stay cool. There are no second chances ... After the storm yesterday I managed about 30 minutes in my bunk as the wind began to moderate, then it was all hands on deck ... Briefly we saw the beautiful full moon, and the wind,

This is real, very real, black and white real, and when you close your eyes that reality does not slip away. There are no second chances

which had been up at over 45, began to decrease ... My sail changes had to start at a time when I scarcely had the energy to feed myself ... Over a period of about 8 hours I did 12 sail changes, from triple-reefed main and staysail to full main genoa ... By the time the wind died to 10 knots at sunrise this morning I was hurrying up and down the decks that were swaying around in a massively confused and violently undulating sea ... each time struggling not to fall over, or be hit by a breaking wave through the nets ... By the time I had to pull out that final reef I was close to breaking ... a cold, tired and emotionally drained wreck. Sitting, checking for hours and hours with every muscle in your body tense – just waiting for the next thing to go wrong takes its toll – even the anticipation of a real arse-kicker storm makes you feel quite weak at the knees ... My mouth was dry, I felt quite out of sorts ... fear and grim anticipation work in funny ways ...

Now I'm here at the chart table, and for some reason I felt like getting this down in an e-mail. I guess somewhere in the back of my mind I know that this will feel better tomorrow – these thoughts will have drifted anyway and faded by the next full moon and the sunset ... Incidentally, it seems a while since we've seen the sun ... another day of sailing through dense white drizzly stormy clouds over a grey powerful sea. The generator's on, so my feet are finally warming – and the kettle's full, ready for lunch ... Got that third reef to put in first, though; we're surfing at 26 knots, and the wind just reached 35. We've sailed back into the front that left us behind ... there really is no rest for us out here ... no rest at all ... I think we'll celebrate our Xmas at New Year ... well, we can always hope. Christmas this year was sadly just another day, albeit a bad one, in the office. At least Mobi and I are in one piece ...

E xx

DAY THIRTY 27/12/04
1 day 6 hours 21 minutes ahead
Fastest solo time to Cape Leeuwin

About 22:15 GMT last night, just as it was getting light here, we opened the next bottle of champagne as we passed Cape Leeuwin. It's the cape on the western side of Australia. There's a long, long way to go to the next milestone, though.

I'm very, very tired, but I guess when you're in a big storm you just have to deal with it; there is no way you can get out. Christmas was terrible, really bad. I spoke to my dad very early on Christmas Day, about 7.00 a.m., because I knew things were going to get worse and I just wanted

to call home. Then I didn't get to ring again until about eleven o'clock at night, when I spoke to Mum and asked her to say happy Christmas to everyone for me because I just couldn't deal with speaking to them all.

To have got through that storm with the boat being OK is obviously a huge relief, but then all your body wants to do is shut down and sleep. But I couldn't because that's when the breeze died, going from 40 knots down to 10 and then back up to 35 over a period of about eighteen hours. During that time I had to change the sails

I'm very, very tired, but I guess when you're in a big storm you just have to deal with it; there is no way you can get out

numerous times, right the way to getting up all the sail that we had and then back down to the least that we could have. Physically it took everything out of me; mentally I was spent anyway. So to go through all of that and then go back into the stronger breeze was just absolutely exhausting. When you get to the end of something like that you're continually asking yourself: 'Am I going to sleep or am I going to eat?' You know you have to do both, and if you don't do one of those things you're going to be in big trouble. It's always that choice – eat or sleep? Am I going to try to close my eyes or try to refuel? It's a constant question.

Sleep has been a huge problem. Commanders are acutely aware of it and I stressed it really clearly to them at the start: we've got to think about wind angles, we've got to think about sail changes, because a sail change is energy, and there is only one of me on board. They're very conscious of it, but, equally, they're not afraid to say, 'OK, we're going to need you in thirty-six hours and you're going to have

to work your arse off, prepare yourself for it.' They're good like that.

We're managing to sit with this front as it moves across to the east, which is great, because it means we're moving at its speed. It looks like we're going to be sitting in it for the next few days, which means we should get relatively consistent wind from a consistent direction. The only problem is that it's more northerly than north-westerly, and we'll suffer a bit more in the waves. But the more consistent breeze should get us to the east without too many problems, and we'll be heading straight down the line of where we want to go. So, from a boat-speed perspective and a gaining-on-the-record perspective, it's perfect. But the weather situation starts to get a bit more complicated – as we've seen so often in this record, you can get twenty-four hours ahead and then a couple of days later you're just three hours ahead, so things are easily lost. Right now, we've got a breeze which is a lot lighter. It's been dropping down to 22, 21 knots in the last couple of hours, although it's still gusting

24. We've been able to stay with two reefs and a staysail, so there's been only one sail change in the last few hours. We've got good boat speed, the boat seems to be trucking along OK, and the sea state is quite a bit flatter than it was. But, though things are looking good right now, it could all change.

I think to be able to sail fast enough – literally, to sail faster than the wind – and get back through a front is a pretty incredible thing to do. The front did stall and slow for a very short period ahead of us, which allowed us to get back inside. We had to average about 22 knots all the way through the storm in order to give ourselves the chance to do that. I think it's only possible with a multihull like *B&Q*

to do that kind of thing and be able to get that speed when you need to. The one thing you've got to be crucially aware of is that you mustn't break the boat: the waves generally get quite large and pushing hard in big waves is what leads to breakages. Trying to make that call, trying to find that line, so you can push hard when you have to – that's the challenge. But it was pretty amazing to sail back through the end of it and to go from having really thick, white clouds, pouring rain all the time, no visibility whatsoever, to a few hours later seeing a cool moon and no cloud above you, and then back into that white cloud again, all over a period of twelve hours. It was extraordinary.

> **We're about to get absolutely hammered by a 50-knot breeze tonight and tomorrow, and that's not going to be much fun**

DAY THIRTY-ONE 28/12/04
1 day 14 hours 15 minutes ahead
1,185 miles west of Tasmania

I'm pretty pleased to have got past the cape, that's for sure, and I've ticked another of the boxes, which is a good sign of progress for the trip. It's a positive indication that you're ahead, but, until that final box, it all counts for nothing. That's how I'm thinking in my own mind – it's great to have passed, it's great to be ahead of Francis, but at the end of the day we've got a lot more capes to pass and a long way to get home. The breeze went up to 36 knots this morning. I spoke to Commanders, and they were adamant that the breeze was going to increase really soon, but then it died to 25 knots. In the end I decided to take the reef out, as we had been sitting there for five hours going 2 knots slower than we could have been. So three hours ago I pulled out the third reef, and we've still got 25 knots of breeze! I should sometimes go with my gut reaction; it's all part of learning. But often they're right, so it's hard. I just felt the wind

wasn't going to increase: we were in a clear bit of blue sky, the clouds had gone, the sea temperature had gone up a bit – which all pointed to the fact that we were going to have less breeze, even though the model was saying 35 knots. We had blue skies for a few hours, but it's gone grey again, which is the first indication that the breeze might increase. At the end of the day, it's only on board that you can see the clouds around you. But when you're exhausted, it's easy to forget that sometimes.

Right now we're doing OK because we're reaching, but we're about to get absolutely hammered by a 50-knot breeze tonight and tomorrow, and that's not going to be much fun. It's going to be a pretty similar situation to what we had during Christmas, so I'm not particularly looking forward to it. The breeze is already increasing, and we're having gusts of up to 35 knots, which won't make for an easy

night or an easy tomorrow. After that, we're going to get to New Zealand, where there's a big light patch – we stand to lose a lot of time there. Francis didn't have the best passage past New Zealand, and it certainly looks like we're not going to either. Commanders are keen that we should not go south amongst the bergs and I agree, I don't think it's the right thing to do. But, looking at the file, I can see that there's a really big light patch sitting right over the gap between New Zealand and the islands further south – and it's really light, we're talking 5 knots of breeze. We could move south now, then gybe and go back up north, which would put us east of Campbell Island but west of the icebergs, squeezing us in between the two. That's certainly another option to consider. Things could still change, though.

Sleep is still the biggest concern as well as making sure everything keeps working. It's very hard in the rough weather even to keep the generator running – I've had to restart it about eight times during the last charge. The rough conditions are moving *B&Q* quite violently, interrupting the fuel supply to the generator and creating an airlock. So I have to keep manually restarting. It makes it hard to rest when the generator's running – I run it almost three hours on, six hours off. That's about seven hours a day when I could be resting but can't because I've got to restart the generator every time it stops. This keeps me really, really on edge. I try to get as many jobs done as I can when the generator's running, so I'm always around and definitely awake for it, but it's pretty frustrating.

DAY THIRTY-TWO 29/12/04
1 day 19 hours ahead
830 miles west of Tasmania

Sitting here at the chart table soaked again ... Already changed clothes twice in the past ten hours – thank goodness for Arry, the air-cooled generator (as I type this he's stopped for the third time in twenty minutes – back in a mo) ... It's been another very hard slog ... Yesterday winds much lighter than predicted – so more sail changes, and the stress of hoping that when you pull the reef out you won't be putting it in just an hour later. Yesterday evening it became evident that there was a storm brewing to the west that was going to hit us hard again – and, as the hours ticked by, it hit worse than the Xmas storm ... We're in it – gusts over 45 knots, and the sea is pretty damn bad, waves breaking all over the place – and the 15m² storm jib seems gigantic. It's been a non-stop night, afternoon and morning, though looking at the clock it's now lunch-time local! Just after dark I put up the storm jib and spent half an hour adjusting the third reef. Both done, now bearing away to avoid the risk of full-on hits with the waves – though there's always the odd one which catches us out ... I got a full frontal wave which completely winded me while I was rearranging the gennaker in its bag – and now that the protective netting's gone, there's a lot more cold spray to hit the face ... Storm jib went up without too many probs – then it was down below to tackle the now three-hour charge, trying to keep other batteries up ... genny stopped again – hold on, OK, on ... I guess if my stomach's in my mouth each time we fall off a wave, then I can't begin to think what's happening to the fuel and oil in there ... just one more washing-machine

The boat's firing down the waves. Probably about every minute we get hit on the side by a wave, which is like a gunshot going off

cycle . . . I got the batteries up to about 70 per cent, which, under the circumstances, was not bad, I thought – then set about checking on deck again . . . Unfortunately the mainsail had filled with a pocket of water – so the next stage was another bear away and a 40-minute fight to pump the water out with the bilge pump. I could hardly stand up on deck let alone hold the pump down and work the handle . . . It took about 20 goes, but on my last one it worked, and I managed to get the sail back on the boom – no longer loaded down with 100 kilos of water trying to rip it apart. On coming below I managed to get an hour or so on the floor after changing clothes again . . . At least I slept – then woke feeling hungry, but this time chose to ignore it and laid my head back on the damp fleece to snooze again. On awakening there

was a 2-hour list of tasks. I bailed out the area beneath the pilot arms, but couldn't work out where the water was coming from . . . Finally I discovered it was from the old main engine bay – and there was about half a ton in there that had come down the old exhaust, which needs to stay open as the air for the generator cooling comes from there. So – I pumped till it was gone – about half an hour. (Generator's stopped again, and a wave just thudded on top of the coachhouse.) So I'm here now having stuffed as much cereal in as I can . . . drank my sports drink dry . . . and will now spend the next 3 hours tending to the generator . . . engineer back on duty! I'm really exhausted, but drying out the boat and creating that list of jobs for after makes me feel a bit better . . . Later on, then.

ex

The tiredness doesn't just come from the storm; it comes from generally sailing the boat. We're currently doing a boat speed of over 20 knots. The boat's firing down the waves. Probably about every minute we get hit on the side by a wave, which is like a gunshot going off. It's a big bang, and you always look to see what's been hit and how hard. There're waves regularly breaking over the windows, and the cockpit's regularly filling with water as waves break over the side of the boat. The motion in the boat makes walking virtually impossible, and you spend a lot of time holding on to things. You're always leaning against something downstairs – it's impossible even to change your socks or stand up inside the boat without getting thrown over – and it's been like that for the entire Southern Ocean and the majority of the Atlantic. So there are lots and lots of things that make actual life on board very stressful, very hard, without the addition of having a storm on top to create problems and water leaking into the boat and all sorts of issues.

Our lead is increasing all the time, and I'm pleased we're just under two days ahead of the record – anybody would be. But I've still got the same mindset that I had on the day I started, and which I'm going to have until the day before we hit the finish, if we make it: it's not over until it's over.

DAY THIRTY-THREE 30/12/04
2 days 15 hours 45 minutes ahead
1,000 miles west of New Zealand

Things are much better now than they've been for the last few days.

We've got a breeze of between 20 and 25 knots, and we've had a good run, averaging over 20 knots at 110 degrees – we're smokin'! I put the staysail down and swapped to solent to go deeper and further south. We've got a nice wind angle of 130 degrees, and, although it's very misty and pretty cold and foggy and the water temperature is down to 6 degrees, we're OK. We're not in a zone with icebergs, but I've got the radar on anyway. I've also had time to do some cleaning up and repairs and get a bit of sleep, so things are pretty good.

We've certainly got a few obstacles ahead of us – one of those includes a light wind area, which is a ridge of high pressure coming down from the north-

It's incredible to look out of the windows right now. It feels as if we're sailing along under a blanket

west. We've got to get through the corner and then out again back into the stronger south-westerlies. But we've also got the iceberg zone to the east of Campbell Island, just south of New Zealand. By sailing into the ridge, I'll come out with a good angle of breeze, which in turn I can use to sail over to the north and try to be clear of the icebergs, fingers crossed. From there we'll head on towards Cape Horn.

I'm going to use the next twenty-four hours to try to sleep as much as possible. I've already done a run of repairs today. The staysail halyard was damaged, and I was lucky it didn't come down – there were only two strands of the Kevlar™ halyard left, that's only one tenth of its diameter. I've respliced that now. It's good to have time to look over the boat and check things. I've got myself a list of things I'm going to do as the weather improves. Some of those I'll start doing tomorrow and some of those I'll do when the wind's a little bit lighter near New Zealand. There are plenty of checks to do; the checks never really stop. But I'll try to use this time to relax as well and switch the brain off. It's been really full on and hard even to eat and sleep, let alone function outside of that, so it will be good just to wind down a bit. I feel on top of things now. Even during the bad stuff, I kept checking, kept problem solving, never putting things off until later. I think I'm

better at that now than I ever have been.

It's incredible to look out of the windows right now. It feels as if we're sailing along under a blanket. The sea temperature is very low, and the air temperature warmer, which leads to thick fog. You can't see anything and the sky has closed in to just a couple of hundred metres away – maybe even a hundred metres. I can see only a couple of wave crests, three at best. To be flying along, averaging 20 knots, with so little visibility is quite unsettling. You try not to think of the consequences of hitting something at 20 knots. At the end of the day, if the radar doesn't see it, there's nothing you can do – just hope. There shouldn't be icebergs here, even though the water temperature is down to 6 degrees.

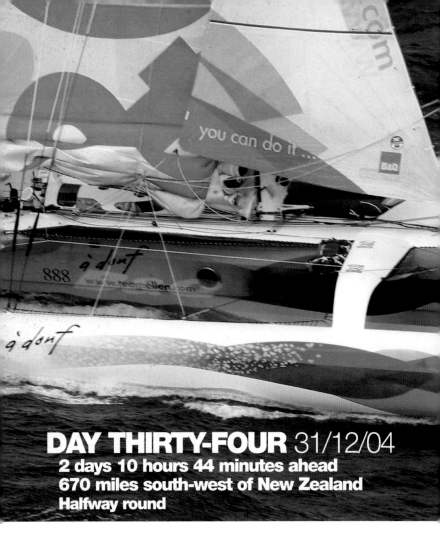

DAY THIRTY-FOUR 31/12/04
2 days 10 hours 44 minutes ahead
670 miles south-west of New Zealand
Halfway round

The objective at the moment is to stay on an easterly course, where the sea temperature should increase. And then, all being well, we'll begin to go north as the wind shifts direction. Right now, it's pretty stressful: the sea temperatures are dropping, visibility is down to tens of metres, plus it has gone dark, so if you see anything then you've probably hit it! There are also quite a few birds around, which is always a sign

of an iceberg. It's hard not to look in front of the boat every five minutes. I really don't want to see an iceberg, especially at this speed. There's a finger of warmer water which we should be sailing into, according to the sea-temperature chart I downloaded. It shows that where we are right now the temperature should be 6.8 degrees. In an hour's time it should go up to 7.4. I just hope that this finger is actually there, because right now the

temperature is going the opposite way, which is not a good sign.

I've not slept since it got light, so probably for twelve hours, and I don't think I'm going to get a huge amount of sleep tonight. We're now north-west of Macquarie Island: it's about 100 miles away and we should be going over the top of it in about four hours. We're averaging well over 20 knots, as the wind speed has decided to increase

on us and the direction's coming back towards the west, which isn't really helping. I wanted to maintain an easterly heading because otherwise we're going to get messed up when we go for the gybe back on to starboard.

I've decided to celebrate New Year on UK time rather than local. And I'm going to celebrate by finally getting my Christmas box out and opening my presents!

DAY THIRTY-FIVE
1/01/05, New Year's Day
**2 days 13 hours 40 minutes ahead
95 miles west of Campbell Island**

New Year has been a lot better than Christmas, there's no doubt about it. We've had a good run, the boat speed has been good, and it's good to come out and have some visibility again. We're still averaging 18 knots; I've got full main and gennaker up. We've been so lucky, we've been just smokin' the last few days, just doing great. And things ahead of us don't seem too bad either: it looks like there's going to be good breeze for the Horn, so let's just keep our fingers crossed and hope.

Right now we have a relatively flat sea, although there is some swell, as we are on the shallows over Campbell Island. There's quite a lot of wildlife around and the sea feels very different. You can sense that you're near the land, even though you can't actually see it. We've got a very grey sky – we've seen no real blue sky for four or five days now. But, all being well, we should be sailing out into a low pressure as the front passes over us, and then we should be in a nice south-westerly breeze which will carry us for the next few days

into the east and the Pacific.

I finally managed to open some Christmas presents – got some great gifts! Not sure what came from whom but guessed a few of them: Oli [Build Project Manager] got me some purple light-up fluffy dice and Loik [Boat Captain] got me a Scooby-Doo nodding dog which is now sitting firmly on my chart table, nodding away! When Scooby nods full on, I will know it's rough!! Lots of other stuff from Mum and Dad, a Christmas pudding – very cool, all very cool. I actually had time to sit and open stuff, which was great.

I think the biggest thought on my mind for New Year is the disaster that's happened in the Indian Ocean and all the deaths and all the trauma that it's caused. I didn't feel anything out here. The sea will have gone up and down without any

doubt, but there's no way you can actually register that on a boat. The fact is, very sadly, that when the wave gets close to the shore it begins to break, just as waves break on a beach, and the difference in height obviously makes a much, much bigger difference on the beach than it does in the middle of the ocean. I found myself just stunned by the news – just not believing that it could have happened. Mentally, I have found it hard to come to terms with the devastation caused by the ocean I am sailing on. I think it has really shocked the entire world, and no one could suffer more than the people who have lost family or friends, and those who lived on the coast. My wish for New Year is that the situation can get back as close to normal with as little pain as possible from now onwards.

DAY THIRTY-SIX 2/01/05
2 days 11 hours 48 minutes ahead
315 miles east of Campbell Island

I've crossed the International Date Line, so am now having the 2nd of January again! I've made a point of collecting food together over the last week so that I don't have to open a food bag for today – I want to avoid opening one for the extra day. I'm judging the number of days I'm at sea by the number of the food bag I'm on, so I'm saving my food bag until tomorrow!

About four hours before sunset today I came across two icebergs, both to the north of me. It did surprise me to find bergs this far north. We passed 70 miles further north than the point of the berg sightings of the Vendée fleet. However, on studying the sea temperature charts more closely, I see that it does make sense – the bergs could have continued on their more northerly route. They were pretty old and melted, and they were sitting in a small corridor of colder water which was moving south–north. The first was kind of triangular and quite small; the second

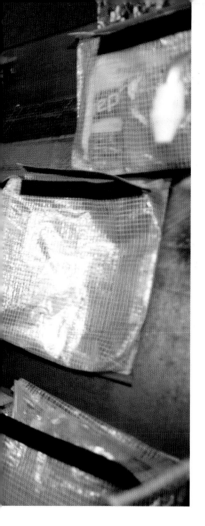

Obviously there is a risk that there could be more icebergs around, although I'm hoping that this decreases with the increase in water temperature

was significantly bigger and had several peaks to it. It was pretty hard to judge how big they were, but I guess they were the size of ships – the second, the size of a large container ship. The water temperature was below 8 degrees. Obviously there is a risk that there could be more icebergs around, although I'm hoping that this decreases with the increase in water temperature.

On the whole it's been a pretty busy day, particularly after having come through the Auckland and Campbell islands south of New Zealand.

We are currently in a south-westerly airflow, which we've been in several times in the south. It changes significantly in strength and is generally very gusty. It's pretty difficult to sail in it, as it's hard to keep a constant boat speed. The wind-speed alarms are going off all the time. But it's a relatively predictable flow that should maintain a similar direction, which is useful for us because it means we can stay on starboard right up until the Antarctic Convergence Zone curves up to the north, about halfway between here and the Horn. We may get away with doing one gybe at the tip of that convergence and then one long one all the way to the Horn. We'll just have to see how it goes.

DAY THIRTY-SEVEN 3/01/05
2 days 12 hours 19 minutes ahead
530 miles SSE of Chatham Island

Well, things have been quite tough over the last few days . . . We're in a very unstable wind situation, and poor *B&Q* has been stopping and starting like there's no tomorrow. The sky is blue mainly, but there are many clouds – some angry, some not – which come in towards us like demons to attack us with their icy gusts. Yesterday we had a few pearlers where the wind reached over 38 knots sustaining 35 for forty minutes . . . The sky went black and the sea a silky grey as the hailstones poured down from the heavens to batter the water's surface. *B&Q* was flying, surfing into the high 20s, sailing deep, down the waves, on the limit – but thankfully not over. I made the most of the second such storm to

collect some spare water, going forward to the mast to hold the bucket under the sail. The water fell – just above freezing temperature – as it melted off the sail. As I watched the storm pass, my skin stung as the hailstones hammered down on us; they clattered off the deck, so they must have been hitting hard – I guess they've fallen a long way! I saved 2

The sky went black and the sea a silky grey as the hailstones poured down from the heavens to batter the water's surface

litres of drinking water, then washed some thermals with the rest – though little smells now as it's so cold, but that will all change when things warm up! Last night we had wind all over the place – and at strengths from 5 to 38 knots. We felt as if we were weaving in and out of the wind – somehow evading it . . . Frustrating and exhausting with so many sail changes [11 in 24 hours]. I managed a few hours of troubled sleep – waking each time to the ear-piercing alarm telling me once again that the wind had risen. I dragged myself off the floor, where I was huddled in my oilskins under a fleece blanket, and looked to the sky to see yet another

demon black cloud.

Though the night was hard and exhausting, there was a really beautiful aspect: sunset was magnificent, with the orange glow lighting up the waves, and the birds around us also lit up by this 'warmth' of light. It's amazing to see the darkest clouds blacken the sky while the boat glows against it, as before a winter's fire. Just stunning. Now that I can see the sky at night, I realize that the dusk just runs into night, and that it never really gets properly dark. In fact, there is always that golden glow on the horizon — dusk melting into dawn, then bringing the new day. At least the nights are

short. This morning things are a little more stable, and the decision is which sails to put up. I'm my own worst enemy in these situations, always wanting *B&Q* to be sailing as well as she possibly can. That's hard in squally conditions, though – hard when the wind speeds are very hard to predict. But I made myself useful,

telling myself to give it an hour or so ... putting safeties on the tramp lashings, bailing out the 3 bucketfuls of water from the windward float. I tried to seal it better this time with silicone. It seems like just yesterday when I was in there bailing out a few buckets. It's a bizarre feeling, sitting with my head poking out of the float –

it's narrow but about as deep as I am tall, so when the hatch is out you can stand on the hull — I felt like a character out of wacky races, my little head jutting out of such a huge graceful shape. I smiled, anyway, but I guess being out here alone kind of does that to you!

ellen xx

I dragged myself off the floor, where I was huddled in my oilskins under a fleece blanket, and looked to the sky to see yet another demon black cloud

DAY THIRTY-EIGHT 4/01/05
2 days 15 hours 45 minutes ahead
Due south of French Polynesia

At the moment we've got gusts of over 40 knots and lightning storms all around us; there have been hail storms all day. Conditions are incredibly unstable – the sea conditions are relatively flat but the wind is just all over the place.

I'm feeling knackered, having had hardly any sleep. The alarm is going off all the time, telling me the breeze is once again over 28, or 35, or 40 knots. It's very difficult to switch off, it's very difficult to wind down, it's very difficult even to stand up in the boat. It's really, really full on, and that's not going to change for another thirty-six hours, so we've just got to hang in there.

DAY THIRTY-NINE 5/01/05
2 days 21 hours ahead
3,020 miles west of Cape Horn

Subject: Here and now – not back then

And I'm back again in the land of the living!! Go, Mobi, go . . .

Hi there, world out there . . . Today I feel a bit like I have awoken into a new world . . . I have an aching hunger inside me which has been absent for a while, and the sea and sky that have been so aggressive are now flat and grey – both. The last three days of sailing have been undoubtedly the worst of my career. Never before have I experienced winds more unstable, more aggressive, more unpredictable.

With a low pressure forming to our NW, we found ourselves getting 'run down' by the energy and cold air rushing north to build it. My body has been pushed to its absolute limits; once again I found myself screaming at the heavens. I'm sure that I've never been as tired as that in my life. Sleep – such an easy thing to say but an impossible thing to achieve in those unstable conditions. Winds have been all over the place – changing in direction by 50 to 60 degrees at times, and changing in strength by 30 knots in the space of

I don't know where the energy came from, as my eyes had been burning red with tears just moments before, but I made a snowman and after that – slowly but surely – everything began to get better

a few seconds. In effect, the worst conditions for a multihull, as capsize is a real possibility – and I have to say that flying along with one reef and the solent in 44 knots of breeze made me talk to myself constantly – I had to keep telling myself that we were in fact going to make it. Yesterday was the worst day, with massive squalls, the same unpredictable wind – the day had begun with a constant 30 knots after a 47-knot gust, and I was sailing with three reefs and the staysail. I'm now full main and genoa. Reefs in, reefs out – body aching. I apologize to the albatross that came closer in wondering what my cries were all about. I was past it, just past it – empty, exhausted. But at that stage, with no escape, no button to push to make everything OK again, no way to hide from the alarms and wake-ups from continuously interrupted dozes – absolute exhaustion. I tried checking the weather out, and, characteristically for the day, the grib I picked up came in six days out of date. I didn't realize this, so that threw me completely, and the end never seemed to be in sight.

But one thing which does, did and will always help is reading the e-mails of support. One yesterday from Oli, one of the team members, who sent an unbelievable mail which could not help but pull you up on a bad day. Thousands are flooding into the website; waiting for the weather to download, I sat there reading people's encouragement, and quite honestly cried. Cried just to see the support of so many people from so many places – it's humbling. I feel like they must be for someone else who is doing something incredible. Yesterday evening the situation changed: I could feel things were improving after the final blast, which was a hail storm. Not just any storm but an inch and a half of sleet in the cockpit. I don't know where the energy came from, as my eyes had been burning red with tears just moments before, but I made a snowman and after that – slowly but surely – everything began to get better. By daylight I was on full main and genoa – and now I have a light breeze – but finally, thank god – a more predictable one.

this is ellen out – about to eat something ...

DAY FORTY 6/01/05
3 days 11 hours 29 minutes ahead
Midway between New Zealand
and Cape Horn

Subject: My life is in your hands ...

I'm sitting at the chart table, my freezing feet braced in the footstraps below. The window just inches above my head is being constantly lashed with spray, and the surface of the sea, which I can see through as it clears, is strewn with white water. We're sailing at an average of 20.04 knots with storm jib and three reefs, and *B&Q* is just blowing me away. This is her moment: she is dealing with what is going on around us with the biggest heart you can imagine. Not just her heart, I feel, but the hearts of the hundreds of people who have put their time, effort and love into building the most incredible boat in the world. I love this boat; she has carried me when I have been tired, as I have cared for her when she has suffered. She is amazing, and right now at this moment I owe, and will owe, my life to her. If only you could see and feel the way she is riding these huge waves – faltering rarely – and just picking herself up after each time she is thrown ... I can't sleep, I'm struggling even to push food down I'm so nervous ...

This is a big storm – and the prognosis is not good – a very real risk of 60 knots, though that's not that much more than the gusts of 47 we've already seen. My feet have remained cold, as I cannot bring myself to get out of my oilskins, and the motion is so bad that I'm constantly holding on to something on board to stop myself getting injured. Things haven't really gone our way in the past few days, with virtually zero recovery time from the last ordeal – but we're still here. For now, we're soldiering on. I'm numb to the tiredness, as my veins are filled with adrenalin and fear. My brain so active it cannot switch off at all ... With my oilskins round my ankles, I lie in the bunk and try to sleep – all I can do is warm up a little and close my eyes, waiting for the next thud as we are thumped by oncoming waves ... Never knowing how big they are is horrible. I find myself lying there wriggling my toes, clenching my fists and – worst – clamping my teeth firmly together. I wondered why: I guess it's either the stress, or the fact that, if I did sleep, I wouldn't bite my tongue with the motion. Things have, to be quite honest, been better. But we're here, we WILL get through this – the Horn is getting closer by the hour.

The support from you all writing in is just mind blowing. I mean mind blowing ... I'm lost for words. I refresh the page each time I log on for the weather and read as many as I can. YOU are unbelievable ...

exx

B&Q is just blowing me away. This is her moment: she is dealing with what is going on around us with the biggest heart you can imagine

888 Rဝ= q'dor

I know the storm is going to be bad,

and I know that every time I charge the
last thing I want is to be messing around
restarting the generator. I've just tried to
do a charge now, and, with the conditions
as they are, it stopped six times in twenty-
five minutes. I can't keep that up. I've got
to be charging six hours a day – I can't be
spending six hours a day running up and
down the boat. It's a complicated
manoeuvre – swapping the main electrical
charging cables, one of which is 'live'. Not

easy with a boat slamming in rough seas,
so I've swapped the air-cooled generator
for the main generator. I need all the help I
can get this week: it's the Southern Ocean,
it's freezing cold and I'm tired, and that's
why I've gone for the main generator.
I managed to burn my arm quite badly on
the exhaust of the air-cooled generator –
I took my shirt off straight away to check
it and it had immediately blistered. I've got
some burns cream in my kit here which
I've smeared on, and it's hurting less.

DAY FORTY-ONE 7/01/05
4 days 8 hours 37 minutes ahead
2,000 miles west of Cape Horn

We've had the worst three days of sailing of my entire career, followed by the most evil of storms, and still we're being hammered. I've done about four sail changes since the storm – we've gone from three reefs and storm jib, to three reefs and staysail, to two reefs and staysail, to two reefs and solent and one reef and solent. One of the biggest issues is that we desperately have to stay to the north, because the more we slip to the south, the worse the breeze will be, the worse the angle will be, and the more we'll have to fight against the wind. The motion of the boat is pretty horrible. I can't switch off, I can't turn my brain off. I haven't really slept for over twenty-four hours, just waiting for the worst of it to pass. I knew the worst was going to be between 22:00 and 06:00 GMT, and I was just bracing myself for it. Until that happened I couldn't switch off; it wasn't safe to. There was only one period at about 21:00 GMT when I managed to sleep for twenty minutes.

I filled my mum's hot-water bottle and got into my bunk and managed to sleep. It wasn't much, but it made a big difference. The rest of the time I just lay there – my feet were freezing, my brain was ticking over, the boat was getting thumped by waves, I couldn't relax. My body was just full of adrenalin, my heart was pumping ten to the dozen, it was really full on.

When we saw the weather report yesterday that came in from Météo-France, saying there could be 80 knots around the centre of this low for a 600-mile radius, it was not one of the best moments of the trip. I have to say, right now, I'm feeling pretty happy to be alive! The fact that we fought our way out of the front of the low, and that we managed to average 20 knots in the last twenty-four hours, means we've escaped the worst of it, and that's where speed can work in your favour. I'm just relieved that we're here with the boat in one piece, and we're heading east. One mistake in the last twenty-four hours and it would have been over for us. The outcome doesn't bear thinking about.

At the moment the sea's not as bad as I expected it to be: the wind is about 20 knots, and we can see some blue in the sky. It seems like forever that we've been staring up at this angry, grey/white, raining sky. What actually happened was that the low developed and produced these very angry north-westerlies before the front went over us. We're going to sail back into it on Saturday, back through the front that

has just attacked us. But, all being well, the breeze will be less strong in the north, and should be more north-westerly and less aggressive.

Cape Horn is just a few days away. We're not there yet, but we're getting closer, and that's a relief in itself, because we've had our fair share of storms down here in the Southern Ocean. We've certainly had our problems, and it's not over yet, I'm acutely aware of that, and I'm not going to drop my guard until we cross the finish line. The next celebration without a doubt is going to be rounding Cape Horn, as long as we get there safely. Cape Horn is the biggest landmark for us sailors:

something lifts off you when you round it, it's definitely something to celebrate. The moment that you actually go around Cape Horn is the moment that you leave the Southern Ocean. There's an element of relief once you're out of the Southern Ocean, out of the storms, out of the isolation. It's an amazing place to sail – it's a place that you're attracted to, drawn to. But it's also very dangerous, and it certainly takes its toll on you and the boat. Although there will still be bad weather, it will never be as bad as the Southern Ocean from a danger perspective, because you're much closer to the land and you're in a different ocean completely.

DAY FORTY-TWO 8/01/05
4 days 17 hours 7 minutes ahead
1,600 miles west of Cape Horn

**We've got over a four-day lead, and I
would never in my wildest dreams
have imagined sitting here,** a few
days from the Horn, with a four-day lead –
just no way. I'm over the moon about it, but
I'm very, very aware that we still have
10,000 miles to sail, we still haven't got
round Cape Horn, and a very ferocious low
is just 250 miles behind us. I'm dealing with
things day by day. Every day I'm trying to
do the best I can. And until we get home,
absolutely nothing, nothing is sealed and
anything could happen. Every single day I'm
thinking: 'What's going to break next, what's

going to go wrong next, what weather
system is going to move differently?'

Ice is still a constant risk; I've got
alarms on the sea temperature. There was
a zone a few days ago where icebergs had
been spotted, and I was on constant
lookout all through the daylight hours. At
the end of the afternoon, I'd seen two
bergs, both quite melted but both to the
north of our position. This was disturbing,
as we were sixty miles to the north of all
reported ice positions. Usually the bergs
would be 300 miles further south, closer to
the Antarctic Convergence, and, with the

temperature of around 7–8 degrees that we have, things should have been fine. I just hope that we're clear of them by nightfall, as they're not showing at all on the radar. It's always a shock to see them, so solid but so silent. At the speed we're travelling, they have the potential to end everything . . .

Francis had a rough time in the South Atlantic – not the first part but the second part – so we can afford to have a few bad days or light days. If we have a lead at the Horn, we could be OK. But Francis had a pretty good time in the North Atlantic; he didn't really see the Doldrums at all because he already had the NE Trades when he was in the southern hemisphere. So, for us, the question is: are we going to suffer in the Doldrums? Are we going to

suffer in the South Atlantic? Are we going to suffer in the North Atlantic? We *could* suffer in all three, we just don't know. The moment you think it's going to be fine, it won't be.

But things will start to change quite soon. Right now conditions are relatively stable, so I'm just hoping things don't get too bad, too soon. Eventually the breeze is going to move behind us again and then we'll be gybing in about twelve hours' time, I think . . . Is that right? No, I can't remember, too hard, too tired. But one thing that's 100 per cent sure is that Monday is going to be an absolutely terrible day. We're going to have very, very strong, incredibly gusty, very unstable winds and I'm not looking forward to that at all.

DAY FORTY-THREE 9/01/05
4 days 20 hours 50 minutes ahead
1,200 miles west of Cape Horn

We've been moving pretty fast, which has led to some exciting sailing.

It's been very rough and the fact that we're so far ahead of the record is a huge credit to Nigel Irens and Benoit Cabaret, the guys that designed the boat. Obviously all the preparations have been important as well, but Nigel's designed an unbelievable boat.

Having this lead is fantastic. It means I can definitely take less risk, definitely push less hard coming up the Atlantic, but at the same time there is also the possibility that you can lose time. Olivier de Kersauson, on a crewed record attempt, lost six days between the Equator and home, so the harsh reality is that it's not over until it's over. You have to decide how much to compromise: how hard do you push and how much do you lose? It's not that straight-forward. We're still 10,000 miles from home, we're in a boat that's getting tired, a skipper that's getting more and more exhausted, mentally and emotionally absolutely zonked, and we've got all the way up the Atlantic to sail. It's not going to be easy, no way. The Atlantic has the lightest winds

on a round-the-world attempt. I feel consumed by the fact; I just can't relax.

Although it's been fast, the conditions over the past twenty-four hours have been relatively stable, so I've been able to get more sleep than I've had in about the last two weeks, although to be honest I'm not feeling that rested. I'm pushing harder than I'd like and I'm not comfortable, but I think it's the right time to push. The longer we can stay ahead of the depression the better – it's only a hundred or so miles behind and catching us up. I've got 21, 22 knots of wind and I'm waiting to take a reef out. I'm trying to rest as much as I can and chill out as much as I can and just look after the boat and not break anything. We don't have to do anything rash, and we've managed to stay in front of this little depression: it's now moving south behind us, which is fantastic news. Now we've just got to sail relatively fast to the east, and the longer we can stay in the north-westerlies the more stable life will be. We can then gybe into the south-westerly flow and head down the western coast of Chile.

Last night, I said, 'Am I going to eat or am I going to sleep?' and in the end I

decided to sleep. I didn't have my dinner until it was getting light this morning, about 4.00 a.m. – spaghetti Bolognese at 4.00 is not good! I ate it even though I really didn't want it. In fact, I almost hurled! I feel like a machine sometimes, working on a rota, and the majority of that rota doesn't even work properly – any bit of it that you can keep working is a good thing. It's hard and it's damn cold at the moment, really cold in the boat. I've only just discovered I can go under my fleece blanket and my sleeping bag, which has revolutionized my sleep! It now takes less than twenty minutes for my feet actually to be 'feelable', which is no bad thing. I have two pairs of socks on the whole time, that's for sure, but if you're active it's OK. After a sail change, you're so soaked with sweat that being cold is not an issue.

The boat's doing OK. The steering system's hanging in there – touch wood – although we broke one of the fuses again yesterday. I've replaced it with a bigger fuse, so we're on our last set, which is slightly worrying with 10,000 miles still to go. But at least we're nearly out of the Southern Ocean – a lot of the trouble that you have with the steering is because the waves are so big and they whack the rudder. The Atlantic should be a little bit less stressful for the system than here.

It feels like we've been in the Southern Ocean for a long time – I'm finding it quite hard to imagine going round the corner. I'm looking forward to it, but I can't believe it's only a few days away, it just feels like that can't be true.

DAY FORTY-FOUR 10/01/05
4 days 22 hours 59 minutes ahead
775 miles west of Cape Horn

As we approach Cape Horn we've got some pretty changeable conditions. We're stuck on the axis of a low at the moment, so we've had the breeze right down to 15 knots, but it appears to be filling in again. It looks like the low has gone through, so our heading is now just to the north of the Horn; it will then move south as the breeze shifts back into the west, which means things don't look too bad. As for an ETA to the Horn, I've no

idea, really. I think maybe Wednesday morning, European time, it's hard to say, it all depends on whether this breeze stays or whether it dies again. I'm hoping it's going to stay; our heading is great at the moment. Let's just hope we can make it to the Horn without too much hassle.

The hardest thing for me is sailing the boat when she feels like she's not going at 100 per cent. I hesitated longer than I probably should have to put the sail up just

because I was concerned about the squall and that's a very stressful thing for me. If the boat's not sailing how she wants to be sailed, I really, really struggle to rest. We've managed to maintain a boat speed of about 16, well, probably 17 knots, which is better than we have been doing. It's slowly increasing, but we're not going to be blisteringly quick. But on the whole we're OK, and it will be a relief to get around the Horn and head north back up to the safety of home. I was on the phone to George at Commanders when we got the first squall. We had only 19 knots of wind, everything seemed OK, no clouds, then we just went off down this wave. I looked out the window and I could see the bottom of the wave – we were at one hell of an angle and it was not nice. A scary moment, on the scale of things. The Southern Ocean is not over; these waves are lethal for a multi. We've got this all the way to the Horn, with maybe 35 to 40 knots when we get there. It's going to be brutal, not fun at all. Trying to work out what sails to have up is impossible. I'm sitting here with two reefs and the solent, feeling like an idiot, as we should have one reef and the genoa to make any decent progress. The squall risk is the biggest danger in these big waves. I've done so many sail changes in the past twenty-four hours that I'm absolutely knackered.

DAY FORTY-FIVE 11/01/05
5 days 8 minutes ahead
380 miles west of Cape Horn

Subject: The Southern Ocean

We're sailing in 30 to 40 knots right now, and getting very close to our gybe just 45 miles off the coast of western Chile. The seas are monstrous, and, as I stand in *B&Q*'s cockpit, I cannot but feel that I shall miss this wild and wonderful place . . . Somehow the south finds places inside you that you were unaware you had; it conjures up the most vivid memories, shows you the most unbelievable and breathtaking sights. Behind *B&Q* there is a rain-filled squall – but from behind this peeps the setting sun . . . the light beams out a rich, powerful, dominant orange over the grey darkness of the clouds, lighting the spray flying from the crests of the waves, giving them a delicate, almost furry texture. How can such a powerful 40-foot wave be so delicate? As the light gets behind a breaking wave, it seems to lift the crest higher . . . the striking turquoise colour makes it seem artificially illuminated from another source – such brilliant colour in an otherwise grey blue sea . . .

A lone albatross circles ahead . . .
How many passing ships has he seen,
I wonder . . . A tear comes to my eye,
because the albatrosses we'll be
seeing on this voyage are now
numbered: their graceful, effortless
flight and constant companionship will
have to remain etched in my mind till
the next time . . .

For, all being well . . . the next
setting sun over *B&Q* will be the last
one in the Southern Ocean, as we
finally leave it behind . . .

                                    ellen x

It's not going to be an easy twenty-four hours, that's for sure. Our approach to the Horn is all over the shop, it's going to be rough. We had a squall of over 40 knots, then 20 knots for about twenty minutes after. We've got a speed that ranges from 15 to 23 knots on average; sometimes it's even below that, which makes it difficult to know when we're going to pass Cape Horn. It's not going to be as early as we thought yesterday. The night has been pretty slow, so I would say between 06:00 and 12:00 UTC. But in the last hour conditions have got a little bit better – whether that's going to stay, I've got no idea, but let's just hope things remain more stable. Whatever happens, we're going to be gybing into the Horn, and there will be a few general manoeuvres to do to get in there – it's not going to be a simple case of turn the corner and hang a left!

Rounding Cape Horn is a huge weight off anyone's shoulders. You are so, so

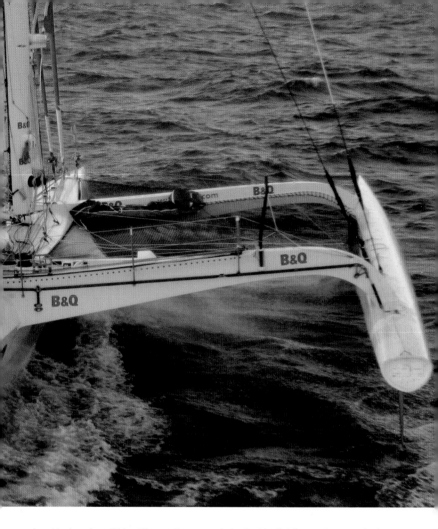

vulnerable down here. We're still several hundred miles from Cape Horn, and it's still a long time before we are round – at least another twenty-four hours. We've just got to take it easy and look after the boat and myself and hope we can get round without too many things going wrong.

The chances of actually completing the trip once you go round Cape Horn go up considerably. You've gone through the Southern Ocean, which is the most dangerous and stressful place you'll sail in

during the trip. But then you've got to look at the other side, at the area where you have the most unstable winds.

What I'm doing out here is just a fraction of what's actually gone into this project. It's an almost insignificant part when you look at the amount of work that's taken place over the last two years, and I feel very lucky to be able to do this part, however hard it is, and to see all these things that I'm able to see. But the support the team gives me is just infinite, it's amazing.

DAY FORTY-SIX 12/01/05
4 days 2 hours 45 minutes ahead
Fastest solo time to Cape Horn

We passed Cape Horn after seven o'clock today, and we've got horrendous conditions. Just before sunset yesterday evening I had to take the mainsail down – we've had up to 50 knots, actually 52 during the night and again this morning. The seas are absolutely monstrous. This morning, as it became light, I realized these are some of the biggest seas I've been in. We've basically sailed over the plateau that shelves to the south of Cape Horn, which means the waves are breaking much more aggressively and have grown to a bigger size – this has

made things really difficult. The boat is getting thrown around like a cork. At least we've got the wind behind us, that's a godsend. The bad news is that there are lulls between the stronger breezes, and the boat gets thrown around seriously in the waves when we slow down.

This marks the end of 12,000 miles of the Southern Ocean, so we should be seeing some calmer conditions, hopefully within ten hours once we've gybed to the north. When we get a little bit behind land, things will start to stabilize. The sea should begin to decrease, and it will certainly be nice to get a bit more sail up.

Even though we've passed Cape Horn, we're still heading south. As I look out of the window, the sea to our port side is awash with white water. A huge wave has just broken next to us, and there must be a 200-square-foot area of sea which is just foaming white water; and then the next wave rolls up and away we go on another crazy surf.

DAY FORTY-SEVEN 13/01/05
4 days 19 hours 53 minutes ahead
70 miles west of the Falkland Islands

I can't believe last night. The wind did a full 360 as the westerly and south-westerly breezes split – impossible to predict and totally unexpected. Last night I got the main back up with three reefs in about 35 knots of breeze, then in the early hours of this morning I sat there with three reefs expecting 40 knots but ended up with just 3! I didn't know what to do – this hadn't been forecast, and I knew that if I put full sail up and we got hit by 40 knots we would be in big trouble. In the end I couldn't wait any more, and I had to go for more sail. It was a massive relief to get round the corner, but it has taken even more out of me. We can't be far off twelve sail changes in twelve hours, and I'm

exhausted, absolutely exhausted. With such light winds, we had to do it, though, there was no choice at all. We either had to sit there stopped or change sails to get the hell out ... I'm a wreck. You don't expect miracles, but I'd hoped for something more stable.

We were escorted for three hours today by a Royal Navy warship, the HMS *Gloucester*, which was amazing. A Hercules from the Falkland Islands and the helicopter which lives on board the *Gloucester* also came past, and then a couple of hours later two Tornadoes flew by and gave us an air show! It was fantastic. It's been great to see people, even though it's through binoculars. It's been a long time, and it's really amazing to think that people have made all that effort just to come out to see me. It's so wonderful; I'm just bowled over.

We passed by the Falkland Islands, which was quite emotional. We made a lot of friends and had a lot of good times the last time we were there just under a year ago. It feels weird not stopping when you know what's there. Still, we have to continue – homeward bound!

DAY FORTY-EIGHT 14/01/05
4 days 18 hours 4 minutes ahead
385 miles off the Argentine coast

Today has not been the best day in the project. We have very light winds and a low very close by. I'm already having to do one or two sail changes every hour to keep moving. The prospects for the next few days aren't great either. We're going to have a terrible time tonight: the breeze is going to come in from the south-west and we should have some fast sailing for a while, but then we're going to head up to a high-pressure ridge which looks like it's going to eat us. We'll have to beat upwind against the wind to get to the Equator, so it looks like we're going to have a pretty bad passage from Cape Horn all the way up to the Equator. To think that just forty-six hours ago we were at Cape Horn, beating our brains out in winds gusting 50 knots, and now here we are in the sun with warm temperatures and no wind. As the wind has been light, I decided to get some tasks done. I've actually had a very productive morning: I bailed the bottom of the boat out, fixed a leaky tap and fixed the steering, so I can now steer without the tiller twisting on its socket.

An amazing thing happened this morning. I was standing a little way up the mast, working on the active echo, when I looked across and there was a huge albatross, the biggest one I've seen during the whole of this trip, and it was right next to me. It flew around the boat; there's hardly any wind, so it was flapping its wings, which you see very rarely. It was just awesome – massive, beautiful, graceful. Its wingspan must have been two and a half metres! It was almost as if it had come to say goodbye from the Southern Ocean.

The corner of the gennaker slipped out of the furler, flew out and hit me on my forehead – it was pretty messy, there was blood dribbling everywhere and I've got a big lump

DAY FORTY-NINE 15/01/05
4 days 5 hours 24 minutes ahead
525 miles NNE of the Falkland Islands

For four hours we've had constant wind, which has been averaging 20 knots, and about two and a half hours ago the breeze kicked up to 24. It feels like it's trying to break the boat to pieces – we're falling off every third or fourth wave. The whole boat is shaking, the main halyard is creaking, everything is groaning, runners are stretching, and there's nothing I can do. I've tried slowing down, I've tried speeding up, I've tried everything, but the fact is we've got mountains heading towards us caused by this low that's sat on our nose. You go over three waves, close your eyes and hope it's OK, then, on the fourth one, WHACK – I'm sure something is going to break. I was trying to sleep, but I decided to try to put a reef in, as we generally reef at 22 knots down-wind. So I put the reef in, and since then

our average wind speed has been 20 knots and our average speed over the ground 15 – which is frustrating, because we should be doing a decent speed and averaging 18 knots with a full main, but we're not. We've got a ridge to get across – it's not like there isn't anything in front of us that we haven't got to get across, there is. It's a barrier, and it's going to get bigger and bigger with every hour, and we've already just lost fifteen miles. It's serious.

To top it all off, the corner of the gennaker slipped out of the furler, flew out and hit me on my forehead – it was pretty messy, there was blood dribbling everywhere and I've got a big lump. I tried to put a plaster on it, but I'm pretty sweaty so it wouldn't stick and I'm going to have to run the generator in a minute, which isn't really going to help.

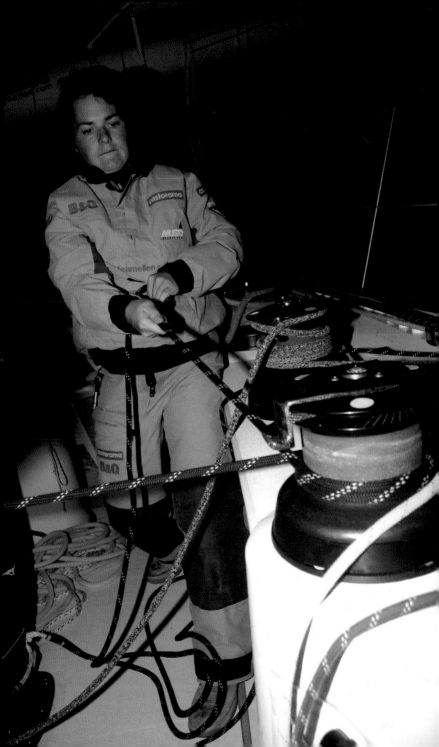

DAY FIFTY 16/01/05
3 days 22 hours 33 minutes ahead
500 miles south-east of Buenos Aires

Subject: Where am I now . . .

It's the morning here, and I'm feeling the most human I've felt for days. Last night, after our gybe and third-reef episode yesterday, I, for the first time, had the boat in a configuration in which we were safe for a few hours. The wind would decrease from its 40-knot gusts – and the terrible sea conditions should – in theory – improve . . .

The last few days have not been just testing, but have taken me once again a long way inside myself to find the strength to keep sailing safely. Since Cape Horn, which seems to me like weeks ago now, I've had nothing but changeable conditions. We've had every sail up, bar the gennaker, and the mainsail through its full range on several occasions. Yesterday I was more tired than I have been on the whole trip – with conditions worsening through the day. My body ached with the strain of the trip so far, my joints throbbed – together with the lump on my head, I just felt like I was empty. I've tried so hard to rest – but when things are changing with the weather and the boat's safety is in danger, it's very, very hard to switch off. Disconnecting the brain does not come easily. Although your body might be exhausted, your brain doesn't seem to allow itself to switch off . . . and though functions like eating, drinking, charging the batteries, coiling the ropes, can become tasks forced by habit, sleeping is not necessarily something that comes on demand. We had a terrible time – the wind building, the seas horrendous, we needed to get east – but the waves were pushing us west. *B&Q* was suffering, and so was I. I made lunch, albeit at about 14:00 and after a frantic gybe in 35 knots, with seas breaking all over the boat (which ripped off the starboard mesh protection!). I climbed straight on to my bunk after putting on a new dry shirt – and thought, 'At least I've eaten, now sleep.' Then I realized that I couldn't remember having eaten – and glanced over to the galley to see my food still sitting there stone cold. I ate it straight away, anyway – followed with some sports drink – but that just shows how tired I really was.

But last night, during a short break in the weather's busy schedule, I was able to get some sleep – how much I don't know, but I forced it. I lay still – I had to – and I do feel a bit better. I'm not back at 100 per cent, but I'm back, looking forward to gybing out of this horrible sea state and pointing our bows once again to the NORTH!!

ex

DAY FIFTY-ONE 17/01/05
3 days 22 hours 33 minutes ahead
600 miles east of Punta del Este

**I need to make gains towards the
north, but I was sat here doing
1 knot for what seemed like ages.**
The boat is shifting again now; I just hope
the breeze continues to head for the north
so we can get the hell out of here. With
only 2–3 knots of breeze, we can't sail
properly. As soon as we get the north-
easters, we'll be in the new breeze and up
to 20 knots, which will give us two hours

to furl the Code 0, get the genoa up and
then go from the genoa to the solent – not
much time to rest. In the middle of the
high the breeze goes round in circles, but
we're not even there yet. The air-cooled
generator is cooking; it makes life in the
boat unbearable. I just want to make the
transition and move on.

Sleep has been very difficult. Loads of
people have been telling me I've got to

sleep, but that's the one thing that you know yourself. You know how tired you are, but when the winds and conditions are changing so irregularly and the seas are bad, it's very, very hard to sleep, and that little bit of grabbed sleep is never enough. It's been good over the last six hours to catch up on a little bit more of sleep, as right now we've got several hurdles ahead of us. We're approaching the coast of Uruguay, where we're anticipating light winds. At the moment we've still got 15–16 knots of breeze, but this will decrease over the next few hours to absolutely nothing. There's also a ridge of high pressure which we'll be going through in the next few hours – basically, there'll be wind one side of it, wind the other side of it, and nothing in the middle. Just twelve hours later we're going to be sailing into an old weather front with a new depression falling down it. Then we've got a depression which is heading across the South Atlantic leaving thunderstorms and goodness knows what behind it, so we've got to try to get behind that depression and through into the breeze on the other side, which is potentially 25–30 knots upwind. It's going to be pretty testing, that's for sure.

DAY FIFTY-TWO 18/01/05
3 days 18 hours ahead
700 miles east of Punta del Este

It was a difficult day yesterday and a difficult night, and today's not looking much better. We passed the high-pressure ridge, which took us hours to get through, as we had no wind whatsoever for a few hours, and right in front of us now we've got an old front which has very change-able winds in it. I'm trying to punch to the north of that at the moment, but the waves are right on the nose of the boat and we're getting thrown around quite violently. All being well, we'll get through to the other side of this and into the upwind conditions of the Trade Winds, where we can actually start to

make some decent progress to the north.

Physically I'm feeling a little better than I did four days ago, but on the whole I'm still exhausted. Since we came around Cape Horn in those horrendous conditions we've had nothing but changeable winds from different directions – we've had all the sails up and down numerous times. We've just got to hang in there and keep moving. It's not been much fun recently, and I'm looking forward to getting into something that's actually close to stable.

This has been one of the hardest stages of the record so far. To have had so many hurdles, as we've had over the last few days since Cape Horn, all in a row, has been pretty brutal. I'm just trying to take every hour and every day as it comes – it's sometimes not a good idea to think about the big picture. There is no doubt we're slowing, there is no doubt we're losing a lot of time at the moment, but we've just got to get through this and out the other side – there is no point in thinking about anything else right now.

DAY FIFTY-THREE 19/01/05
3 days 4 hours ahead
720 miles east of Porto Alegre, Brazil

The South Atlantic has not been kind to us; nothing has been easy since Cape Horn. It seems like we're chasing a front that's moving away from us, we're going nowhere. This is a very hard challenge and there are very few relaxing moments. The boat is never still, even with no wind; it is always banging and crashing.

At Cape Horn it really looked like the record was possible, but with every day that goes by it's slipping away from us. All that effort, all that energy, seems wasted.

Twenty-four hours of fighting to get through something that is moving along at the speed that we are – in both cases, very slowly. We need wind to get through this cloudy barrier, but the wind itself is the other side of it. It feels impossible, like we'll be trapped here for weeks continually changing direction, continually adjusting to the unpredictable clouds we have. But I'm not going to give up. I've given everything and I feel empty, but I'll find that little bit left in me to get us through the last 5,000 miles.

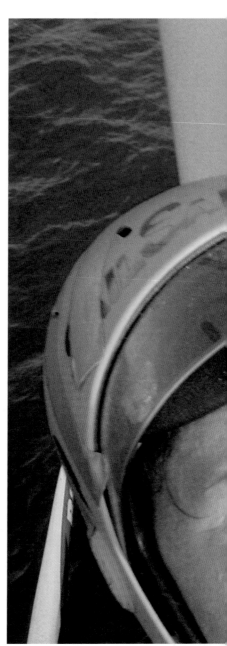

DAY FIFTY-FOUR 20/01/05
2 days 14 hours ahead
890 miles ENE of Porto Alegre, Brazil

Though the front was a huge struggle, it paled into insignificance this morning. My heart was in my mouth. We had a serious problem with the headboard car. I took it down but had to go up the mast to assess the damage at each reef point where it had ripped off and damaged the mast track. It had broken in the early hours of this morning – the crayons came out and pulled it off. I think the headboard car system broke during the night. In the end I climbed the mast twice, the first time to the second reef, the second time to the first reef, which is not far from the top – a long way up. My body felt shot before I even did the climb. The conditions were also pretty terrible, but I couldn't think about that because the job needed doing and in order to keep up with the record I had to do it as fast as possible. So I just had to get on with it. But it was physically very, very tough. It's not flat water at all, we've got 20 knots of breeze, and all movement at the top of the mast is magnified hugely. I found myself being hurled against the mast again and again, and trying to prevent my head, or my elbows, or my legs, being hit on the rig. But you can't stop it happening. It's impossible because you're thirty metres in the air. Not much fun at all! The damage at the first reef was not too bad, not like the second reef. It was badly damaged and burred. I cut my thumb while I was up there, which made me laugh ironically, as I thought to myself when I saw it bleeding that the doctor's advice would be to keep it elevated. At over thirty metres up, I can't

do better than that! I can't believe what I've been through in the past two weeks, I'm buggered. It was all I could do to hold on, it was brutal, really hard. And to cap it all, this morning, after discovering the mast problem but before making the ascent, yet another Royal Navy ship, HMS *Endurance*, heading south, passed by. I experienced strong conflicting emotions – real joy in seeing the crew on the deck waving and cheering, but then in an instant, when they had gone, I was plunged back into despair at the thought that our whole record attempt was in jeopardy. But the job's done now, and it's the best feeling this evening to know that we could actually put the full mainsail up if we needed to. I don't think the timing could have been worse: I'm absolute toast. But we did it, we've made it, and we're moving again. In one sense it's a godsend that it happened. It made me realize that however badly we're doing, or will do, against the record, if the boat and I are in one piece, we still have a chance. A fighting chance.

DAY FIFTY-FIVE 21/01/05
1 day 20 hours ahead
770 miles ESE of Santos, Brazil

I feel like I've been beaten up. I'm aching all over, stiff as hell, and moving round with the speed and elegance of an arthritic robot! I've got massive bruises on my left leg from where it was jammed between the sail and the mast. Every muscle in my body feels like it's been torn. I'm glad I went up again yesterday – if I had had to go up today, I wouldn't have done it, I couldn't have done it. It was the right thing to just go up yesterday evening and get it over and done with while I was 'adrenalized', as it were. I'm pretty happy that I've managed to make a repair and been able to carry on with the record without too much setback in terms of miles. The mast track is now fixed satisfactorily; the car can go up and down. It's not 100 per cent – there's a risk when I have the second reef in, as I do now. But

I'll just have to learn to live with it – there's not a lot I can do about it. We've got to hang in there and do our best and hope that it doesn't give again. It's just been one big mission, and I'll certainly be pleased to get across the Equator.

We're going to lose time, without a doubt, in the next twenty-four hours, in fact the next thirty-six hours, because of the light winds ahead. I stood on deck earlier and shouted out to the sky that I couldn't do another sail change. We're beating upwind, which is the slowest point of sail. It's not ideal; no one wants to do this because it's not fast. But, unfortunately, it's all we're left with. We're now going to sail into a high-pressure ridge again – very slow, very painful, very hot and very frustrating. Only when we come out of the other side of that ridge will we get into the Trade Winds, and then, in theory, we should have the most stable winds that we've had in about sixteen days.

We're going to be in pretty bad shape at the Equator, because we have to go through tomorrow with very little wind. But I believe we can still set this record. If I didn't, I would go to Brazil right now! Until the second hand ticks down and there is no time left, we can still do it.

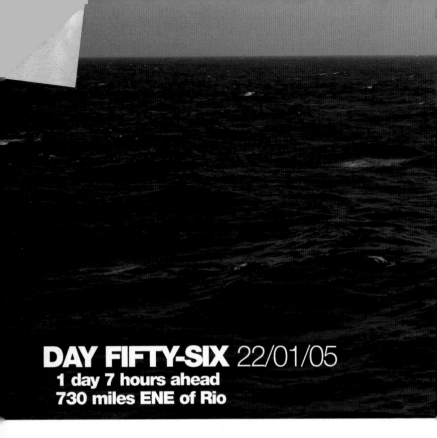

DAY FIFTY-SIX 22/01/05
1 day 7 hours ahead
730 miles ENE of Rio

The South Atlantic has been terrible for us, absolutely terrible, worse than I've ever experienced before, especially as it's been so unpredictable. Francis had a pretty bad run up the Atlantic, but nothing like we've had. We were four days ahead of him at Cape Horn, and if we cross the Equator ahead of him, it will be a miracle. It just sums up how horrendous the South Atlantic has been. From Cape Horn onwards all I've really been after is some stable winds for twelve or twenty-four hours, just something to give us a chance to recover, but it's not come. There's been nothing, not one day when things have been all right. There've been lots of sail changes: I've had the mainsail up and down many times since Cape Horn – probably more times than the whole of the Southern Ocean put together – and it's been pretty hard work. Physically it's been shattering, and obviously the problem with the mast track the day before yesterday was just horrendous.

Getting into the Trade Winds, having a breeze in which we can sail relatively quickly and make good progress to the north, is going to be a relief. We've still got the Equator and the Doldrums to come, but that could work in our favour, it could be OK, or we may get stuck there, we just don't know. Let's just hope there are fewer obstacles in the North Atlantic than we've seen in the South. We're currently heading on an ENE course into the centre of the high pressure. We need to make some ground north, because north is home. But

I'm also concerned about Trindade Island approximately 75 miles north of our position. If we tack to the north now, we're going to end up tacking back and getting closer to the island, and I'm worried about the wind shadow that the peak of the island may cause.

Last night I spent at least two hours up on deck because there were ships going past and I didn't want to go to sleep with them around. But I did get some kip and I also managed to get some jobs ticked off this morning. So at least I feel like I'm getting on top of things.

Right now, I feel achy, very, very tired and a bit relieved that we've got some light winds and a stable boat so I can recover a little bit. At the moment we have about 7 knots of breeze, which is great, but it's not going to last very long, things are going to get worse. I just feel absolutely empty – it has been a real struggle from Cape Horn to here – every day has given us new challenges. And now I'm going to have three days of basically no wind, so we'll be going very, very slowly and we will almost certainly lose the lead.

I keep going because this isn't something that just sprang out of the dark. Building the boat and working on the project has been in my mind for a long time; it's not just something that started the day I left from Falmouth. However hard it gets, that knowledge doesn't let me go. This record attempt, right now, is the object of all our efforts.

DAY FIFTY-SEVEN 23/01/05
13 hours ahead
1,270 miles south of the Equator

Our five-day lead has been whittled away to less than a day now, but we can't give up just because we've had a few days of light winds. I think we'll probably be significantly behind Francis when we cross the Equator. At the moment, though, we're still a couple of weeks away from running out of time. The South Atlantic's been horrendous; we've lost four days in a period when Francis was very slow himself. But the North Atlantic's still to come, and, if all goes well, then we do still stand a chance. Obviously if the weather's against us, then we're scuttled. Right now I'm on an absolutely flat sea – it's one of the flattest I think I've ever seen. There are no waves. It's just flat with a few little ripples on the water whenever there's breeze, and on my starboard side I can see the island of Trindade, which hopefully, all being well, we're going to pass and leave on our starboard side. We may have to tack to miss it, but at the moment it's still thirty miles away.

I seem to have found some kind of inner peace tonight, and, though today has been a very hot and little restful day, I feel surprisingly good

Sometimes you feel the need to write but aren't sure why ... Now is one of those moments. The sun set a few hours ago over the most unbelievably flat sea ... it seems strange not to feel *B&Q* being tossed around by the waves, and her every move dictated by the waves around her. Now we're surrounded by a lightly textured, slightly undulating carpet, which stretches farther than the eye can see by thousands of miles. I seem to have found some kind of inner peace tonight, and, though today has been a very hot and little restful day, I feel surprisingly good. The weather could not be worse for the record: as I sit here we're sailing at 4 knots. But we have what we have; we cannot alter the weather. It's true that the South Atlantic for us has been absolutely terrible. We couldn't have had more changeable or worse conditions – but we need to remember that we're here. We could be in worse shape and we're here. It's better to forget the 4-day lead we had at the Horn and think about each day as it comes. Do the best we can – then the rest will happen on its own. We've pushed hard and given our maximum, and will continue to do so – time will

bring the outcome ... not tears, frustration or stress. Easy to say, but tonight I feel in control – which is better than how I've felt the past few weeks. I think mentally it always helps me to get on with jobs on board, and today I tinkered away in the scorching heat, as it was too hot to sleep anyway. I rewired both ends of the earth protector for the active echo, checked the steering bearings, replaced some protection on the mast, removed the damaged netting protection from the port side, checked all the seals on the float hatches, fixed the fixings in position, epoxied the bull's-eye back on the deck for the solent, and also bonded the deck that had been torn up as it went flying. Checked the diesel levels – all OK, you know – the usual Sunday 'maintenance'! All in all a good day's tinkering. Anyway, the wind is all over the place and I'm horrified to see that it's doing its best to plague me with the stress of which sail. A light and variable wind which is 90 degrees from where it should be coming from. The usual – more challenges.

signing off from a humid cabin ...

exx

Slinky did his best to
keep me smiling

DAY FIFTY-EIGHT 24/01/05
0 hours ahead
650 miles south-east of Salvador

We have finally lost our lead. I'm hanging in there, trying to bear in mind that it's just for another two weeks, and that if we're not back by then it doesn't matter anyway. That's the way I'm thinking and I'm trying to look after myself the best I can. I'm exceptionally tired, pretty exhausted and fairly bruised. I've been up the mast again this morning to do a rig check, so I'm feeling pretty battered.

It feels like a new race every day. No matter where you are, ahead or behind, you've always got to treat every new day with respect. You've got to get the most out of the boat and yourself as you can, and I've done that every day through the race, even when we had a five-day lead. And I'm very glad that I did push that hard, even with that lead, because if we hadn't, right now we'd be a long way behind the record. So, for me, every day's a new day, and the record is definitely still within our sights – I'm not going to let go of that. I've been at sea for over fifty days, and now is not the time to throw my hands up in the air and give up, no way. We're level with Francis – we're not three days or five days behind him. But we only have a chance if the weather is kind to us.

I'm trying to be positive, although it's been exceptionally difficult: it feels like everything has been against us. And losing our lead on Francis in a period when we should have gained is hard to come to terms with. But what can we do? We can only do our best and we can't do any more than that. So I've tried to occupy myself by fixing things, getting everything back on track.

It's been amazing to see the amount of support from people – people writing into the website saying that they have been praying for good winds, wishing the breeze will come back – it's been absolutely incredible. And if ever there was a reason not to give up, it is that so many people are behind us. I don't feel like I'm alone out here; there are a lot of people wishing this boat along. Things could be a lot, lot worse.

If ever there was a reason not to give up, it is that so many people are behind us. I don't feel like I'm alone out here; there are a lot of people wishing this boat along

It's calm outside as we spend another 24-hour period on this incredibly flat sea . . . It's a strange sensation to be out here, still with the clock ticking but at the same time feeling utterly helpless and unable to make a difference. Here we have light winds, and that's that . . . We can sail our optimum upwind – and that's the best we can do for now . . . It's actually quite beautiful, and having just a little time to rest and recover in stable conditions has probably done me the world of good before what I'm sure will be a stressful, stormy and tense final two weeks . . . *B&Q* is as ready as she will ever be – I have checked and rechecked, and am almost certain that we can do no more . . . I'm OK – I think I've managed pretty well to de-tune a little and find myself again after the last few weeks of near exhaustion . . . That's a good thing, I guess, that has come out of this . . . It's incredible to think that we've been out here for almost sixty days, and that Xmas and New Year are all behind us . . . It seems like only yesterday that we slipped our lines from Falmouth, seen off by a fantastic flotilla of boats . . . but on the other hand it feels like life on board is almost all I know now, and that readjusting to another life – 'the' other life – will be hard . . .

But, hey . . . we're still a couple of weeks away, so life here goes on . . . In some ways I really am looking forward to finishing, to seeing everyone again, those I've been apart from for almost two months. But I think the main draw to the finish is to finally end the worry, pressure and strain that my mind and body are under right now. It's the not knowing – how we'll finish, what will break – that's what takes its toll . . . Take the record away, and it simply becomes a voyage around the world; add the record again, and it becomes a very real and very arduous race – a race against time, my invisible competitor . . . but above all a race against my own capabilities and myself . . .

exx

DAY FIFTY-NINE 25/01/05
10 hours behind
600 miles ESE of Salvador

It's been unbelievable. I've never,
ever sailed in conditions like these.
Never. Never. Never had four days of
nothing – it's just a wide, open, black
space with a little breath of wind every
now and again. It's such a change from
what we've been living with for the last
two months. It's amazing. You couldn't
wish for a more beautiful place to sail.
We've got 8 knots of breeze, we've got
a boat that's slipping along at 9 knots,
we've got a beautiful moon, the most
beautiful I've ever seen, it's just incredible.
You never get to live moments like this,
when the sky's completely clear and the
sea's flat and the moon rises and it's huge
and white, and it's so bright that it lights
the whole sea up. But the timing of this
tranquillity isn't ideal, and I have to try
to allow myself the chance to really
appreciate it.

Not knowing is what makes it so
difficult. Right now, we're going slowly;
the forecast isn't going to allow us to go
anywhere fast, and we just don't know
what's going to happen. There's a huge
question mark – how fast can we get to
the Equator? The faster we get to the
Equator, the better the Equator crossing
will be. The slower we get there, the worse
it's going to be. Everything's a question
mark. You worry all the time: will we get
stuck in the Doldrums for thirty-six hours?
What does the northern hemisphere hold

for us? What's going to break? What's
going to go wrong? Are we going to get
through the Doldrums? Are we going to
run into a high pressure? We just don't
know what's going to happen. All these
questions . . . so much rattles around in
your head twenty-four hours a day.

I think I'm dealing with it OK, trying
to be philosophical, and having some
sleep really does help on that front.
We're getting closer to the finish, and
I've just got to do the best I can in the
time that's left. I want to feel like we're
going home, and, right now, we're still
three days away from the Equator. I keep
telling myself it's not over, we only need
to break the record by a second.

I've put everything into this record –
my heart, my soul, my flesh, my blood,
just everything. I've never pushed this
hard, I've never driven myself so hard,
I've never got so close to the edge for so
long – never, ever. It's been a real roller
coaster – I really had to grunt up, and it's
not over yet, we're not there yet. When we
get north of the Doldrums, I'll start to feel
happier. It's like an oven in here, so I'll be
glad to get into the northern hemisphere,
where things will cool off a little bit.
Whatever happens, at least conditions
will become easier to live in day to day.
Soon we should have the NE Trade Winds,
and, even if they aren't that strong, it
should be relatively fast sailing.

DAY SIXTY 26/01/05
6 hours ahead
640 miles south of the Equator

It's been a pretty full-on night, and I'm really nervous and wound up at the moment. We had really changeable conditions last night, and the motion of the boat sailing upwind was awful – really aggressive and uncomfortable. I've had 23 knots of breeze and am sailing virtually upwind to try to keep the course. There have been loads of clouds around, and I had to dodge a huge fishing boat earlier. Now we've got a little bit less wind and the sea is a bit better, but the breeze is up and down all the time. I've got the right sails up at the moment – I shook the first reef out this morning – so at least we're moving. We're soon going to be reaching on the south side of a low, and that's going to be uncomfortable a lot of the time. I desperately don't want to break anything.

There are a lot of new noises because we've not sailed like this for a while. It's weird to hear all the noise the boat makes when we're bouncing around. I am so, so worried that something is going to go wrong. I spent half of last night on the deck trying to work out where the noises were coming from, worrying about what was going to break next. And there's no doubt we'll have problems, and breakages, between now and the finish. But I have no idea what those will be, so I'm just concentrating on keeping the boat together, keeping myself together, and getting home as fast and as safely as possible. We're coming into the final straight line, and I just feel a huge amount of pressure. I need to try to de-stress and calm down a little, but it is exceptionally difficult to do that when you've got the Doldrums in front of you.

I definitely have to give a gift to Neptune when we reach the Equator, and I'm having a think about what the most precious thing I have on board is. I'm sure that'll become clear in my own mind as I get closer, but it's got to be something very precious and very important, because we really need his help in the final stages.

DAY SIXTY-ONE 27/01/05
1 day 5 hours ahead
Fastest solo time to the Equator

I feel better today – at least we're moving now, thank God. We're a day and a bit ahead again now, so let's see if we can keep something in the bag and get home safely. We have a very, very long way to go – there are still thousands of miles, it's not like it's just round the corner. I'll be glad when we get into the northern hemisphere and across the Equator. We have a steady breeze at the moment, so it looks like

we could well be across the Equator by midnight, but it all depends on whether we lose the breeze when the SE Trade Winds meet the NE Trades, effectively cancelling each other out. After that we've got to try to cross the Doldrums as soon as possible. They're sitting at the moment at about 3 or 4 degrees north, and we have to get across as fast as we can so that we don't fall into the hole which is developing there. All

efforts at the moment are on sailing as fast as we can to the north, and all being well we should get through before it gets too bad. But obviously things can always change, so we have our fingers crossed.

I go through waves of feeling really stressed and nervous, and then waves of feeling a little bit better. But on the whole I think I'm OK.

We had a booby visit us today! I think it was a masked booby. They live only in the equatorial area – it's like a slender gannet with a dark head. They're real characters, and it says in the bird book they don't normally follow boats. This one stayed

We have a very, very long way to go – there are still thousands of miles, it's not like it's just round the corner

with me for three hours. He flew around, and he dived behind me, and he kept soaring around the rigging, getting really, really close. So I had my own pet booby for three hours! It was a beautiful specimen and very exciting to see, and slightly cartoon-like in its behaviour.

DAY SIXTY-TWO 28/01/05
1 day 13 hours ahead
104 miles north of the Equator

We crossed the Equator late last night. It felt like a huge relief to cross the line and to be in the northern hemisphere. I felt incredibly happy for a number of hours, and now I'm back to the reality of going upwind in lots of wind and trying to get the boat home. I decided on Neptune's special gift. I have a little silver charm that I've worn around my neck for some time now. So I thought that might be a suitable gift. Thank you, Neptune, for letting us get this far. We've crossed the Equator for the second time. Let's hope we're going home for a record.

We had a decent breeze when we went across, and we actually lost the breeze for only a few hours in the Doldrums. Late yesterday evening the Doldrums moved south over us, and we managed to get to the north side of them. This morning we have a huge amount of breeze, about 18 knots. We don't know where it has come from, but it's fantastic, and it appears that we've managed to cross very, very quickly. I would say there is probably an 80 per cent chance we're through the Doldrums now. Miraculously, a huge cloud bank dissolved in front of us, which would have meant serious thunder and lightning.

Looking ahead, I think the biggest hurdle we'll have is the high pressure which is hovering around the western approach to the English Channel. The movement of that high pressure will dictate whether the record is breakable, and if it decides to eat us up and sit over us or, even worse, sit over the finish line, we could be in big trouble. But if that high pressure helps us and is situated in a reasonable position that allows us to sail into it and out of it, or indeed round the west side of it, then that will help us enormously. So our destiny really is in the hands of the high-pressure system. We've still got 3,000 miles to go, which is one seventh of the whole trip.

DAY SIXTY-THREE 29/01/05
1 day 10 hours ahead
680 miles SSW of the Cape Verde Islands

We're getting closer to the final stretch now, and things going wrong have a higher price tag on them. It's certainly looking like the finish should be relatively quick, but it all depends on that high-pressure system, on where that's going to move when we get up there, so we've got to try to navigate the best and fastest possible way around that, just to see how quickly we can make it into the mouth of the English Channel.

I can't relax at all – the boat is crashing around and slamming into the waves. The boat's motion in these waves is really bad. I'm so scared we're going to break something, but I just don't know what I'm going to do. I don't think going any slower will make any difference whatsoever – I don't really want to put the second reef in because I've no confidence in the second

reef point. I've got exactly the right sails up at the moment, but it's still pretty stressful.

There is a creaking noise coming from the mast which is worrying me, but there is nothing I can do about that either. I've got the headboard car in the best position possible on the mainsail track, and if it's going to go, it's going to go. I feel I've done all I can, so I've just got to keep on trucking and see what happens. I might be able to drop the sail right down and put the second reef at the very bottom of the mast section, just to be on the safe side. But the biggest thing is not really the load on the mast but the movement, as we slam into the waves. Every time we fall off a wave, the car on the mainsail track goes up and down, and every time the car goes up and down, it grates a bit more off. The worry that something will give just eats away at me.

I saw a whale today! It was very, very close to the boat, and it was just in front of us. We sailed right over it. I braced myself for a collision, to be honest, because it was so close. It went underneath our starboard float and, as it did so, it blew its lungs out, and its back came out of the water. I didn't see its tail, but it must have been over thirty feet long.

DAY SIXTY-FOUR 30/01/05
1 day 12 hours ahead
470 miles south-west of Fogo,
Cape Verde Islands

I hit something last night – I don't know what it was, maybe a fish or squid, I don't know, but it wasn't huge. It got stuck on the leeward rudder, so I ended up turning the boat full circle to get it off. I gybed the boat, the rudder just lifted out of the water and whatever it was came off and drifted away. It wasn't massive, maybe the size of a bin bag, but I really felt the thud.

The high pressure doesn't appear to be moving quite how it was yesterday, so we'll probably end up going upwind into it, rather than downwind through it. Conditions are pretty much going to stay

They say that there's snow in the Canary Islands. First time ever. If that's the case, then I think I'd better get the extra pair of thermals out now

like this for another couple of days – it's still Trades and we're going to start reaching soon. There's a lot of changeable breeze at the moment, pumping up from 14 to 18 knots. The boat's pretty powered up, but it's hard to get the sails right. We always struggle to have exactly the right sails up – we're over-powered rather than under-powered right now, and I'm not sure which is worse. I'm happier with the full main anyway, just because of the car situation, so if I can hold on to full main I will.

I have one layer of thermals on again. It's a really nice temperature at the moment, but I think I might need to get the second pair out in a few days. They say that there's snow in the Canary Islands. First time ever. If that's the case, then I think I'd better get the extra pair of thermals out now, because we're going to be passing Cape Verde soon. We're due to be west of the cape in about sixteen hours, I reckon. And in just over two days, we'll be due west of the Canaries. We should be a bit faster by then.

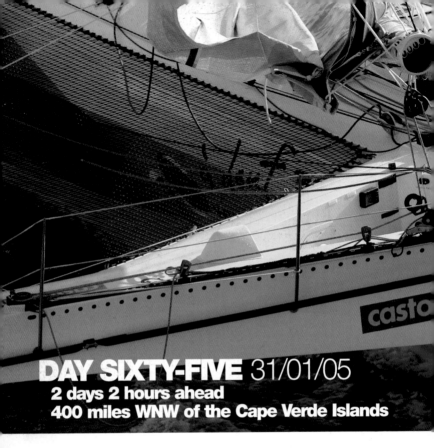

casto

DAY SIXTY-FIVE 31/01/05
2 days 2 hours ahead
400 miles WNW of the Cape Verde Islands

We've got a narrow lead, but all I can do is push as hard as I can for now without breaking myself or the boat. I think we've got a chance of maintaining the lead for a while, but the high-pressure system is still an issue. At the moment it's moving every day, and we don't know what its position's going to be: it could mean we finish with fantastic conditions downwind or we finish upwind with 35 knots, which is a boat-breaking scenario. There are all sorts of different possibilities right now, and no one has the answer. I've just got to keep going and do my best.

Conditions were presumed to be stable, so yesterday afternoon I put the first reef in again. Even though I wasn't sure what was going to happen to the weather, it seemed the right thing to do at the time. I tried to get some sleep. The breeze died to an average 16 knots, then it started raining and the breeze died to 7 knots – the forecast was for it to be in the high teens, maybe twenties – then all of a sudden it was punching up to 21, 22 knots. A second set of clouds came over and the breeze was up to 25, gusting 26 knots, and it averaged that for about six hours. It slowly died down, and now it's gusting 22–23, so it was a pretty unexpected and brutal night. The motion in the boat has been really awful. Because we're now going to start heading into the

Trade Winds, heading east of north, the swell from the Trades is right on our nose. We don't have an option: we've just got to go with it, so here we go.

I'm sailing with the second reef in at the moment, but I've got the headboard car right at the top of the box and I think it's probably OK. I can't hear any weird noises. If we do lose the crayons again and the track is ripped off or damaged, the best place that could happen is at the top of the second reef, not at the bottom. So that's why I've pushed the car to the top – I've put it above all the damage. To be honest, it's very close to the reinforcement. If it screws itself again and rips off, at least we can get back to

two reefs, which is not an insignificant amount of sail.

My hands are so hard and so tight and so rotten . . . they look quite disgusting! There is white rot underneath all my fingernails, and I can chew bits of the skin off without feeling a thing, it's that hard and knackered. We're getting a bit closer every day, bit by bit, and as long as the wind keeps blowing we'll make it home one way or another, if we don't do anything stupid, that is. But I still feel pretty nervous, pretty tired, pretty empty. We've just got to keep things together and get to the finish line, but we've still got a week of sailing, and a week is a significant portion of this trip round the world.

DAY SIXTY-SIX 1/02/05
3 days 6 hours ahead
700 miles WSW of the Canary Islands

It's great to be three days ahead again, but I'm taking each day as it comes. We're having a good run right now; Francis also had a good run at the end. It's swings and roundabouts, and as we get closer the difference is going to matter to a much greater extent.

We have good conditions right now, but after tomorrow things will change very quickly, and we're going to end up in the high-pressure system – this will probably be upwind, so our speeds are going to drop incredibly. I think I just have to be realistic and do my best. I've got to sail the boat as best I can, and the result will be visible with time. There is nothing more I can do; there's no point in me sitting here saying I'm going to break the record,

centre, and it's moving around all the time.

As we head into the high, we'll get the sun back, but the wind will go light and we might have to gybe around the top of the high, go through all the sail changes possible, and then sail upwind to the finish. It doesn't fill me with joy to think of the sail changes – every muscle and joint is hurting. It's hard to imagine being in much before the record at the moment.

I'm looking forward to the finish, to feeling that I can switch my brain off. It's been so intense and concentrated over the last few months that not having to look at the sea or the wind, or think about the batteries, or look after myself to the same extent that I've had to over the last couple of months will be a relief. It's going to be fantastic to see the team and my friends and those people who have supported me. But, right now, the relief is the one thing I'm looking forward to more than anything else. Life out here is incredibly stressful but also amazing. The priorities are different. And, although I have no control over the weather, I have complete control over the boat – she's my responsibility, and I know that as soon as I cross the finish line, whether I have a record or not, that control will vanish. Life is going to change in a very dramatic way.

because quite frankly there is a very good chance I won't, so I've just got to just do my best and see what happens.

Right now, I'm sailing with blue skies on a heading just to the east of north, roughly about 600 miles south of the Azores. Things have been pretty tough since Cape Horn: we've had no wind or Doldrums or difficult conditions. But on the whole I feel pretty happy to be where we are, happy to be sailing at the speed we're sailing. The worry is still there, though. There's a high-pressure system sitting in front of us with no wind in the

DAY SIXTY-SEVEN 2/02/05
3 days 10 hours ahead
330 miles SSW of the Azores Islands

I eventually slept in my oilskins in the cuddy. It was in-and-out-of-consciousness sleep, rather than solid sleep

I didn't get much sleep last night at all; it was rough, and the breeze was up and down like a yo-yo. The breeze would die to 14 knots, and then within two seconds it would kick up to 28, and then within a minute it would die back down to 14 again. The forecasts are a bit of a waste of time right now; the weather models bear no resemblance to what we have. I just can't get any sleep, because every time I get the sails right and I think I can rest, the alarm suddenly goes off and there're 27 knots of breeze again.

I eventually slept in my oilskins in the cuddy. It was in-and-out-of-consciousness sleep, rather than solid sleep. I lay down on the bunk for an hour again this morning, but I couldn't sleep at all. I was getting thrown against the side of the boat, and the alarms were going off.

I don't know whether to change up to the solent – I'm now on two reefs and a smaller staysail – it's right on the limit in the gusts, but I've got only 18 knots right now. I need to be going faster, but the sail change takes twice as long as it did earlier in the trip because I'm so much more tired now. And I don't want to risk breaking the solent. The problem is that we have to make more gains now, as the weather looks terrible ahead. Current routeing shows me in late Tuesday, and the trend is getting worse. Now is the only time to make gains.

DAY SIXTY-EIGHT 3/02/05
3 days 6 hours ahead
15 miles east of Terceira Island,
Azores Archipelago

I can't believe what we've been through. We stopped for two hours with two knots of breeze from the wrong direction. The breeze went into the north-west, and we were heading back towards the island, only fourteen miles away. We've moved some, we've stopped, we've talked about tacking, we've taken reefs out, put reefs in, we've had 22 knots, then we've had 4 knots, then 19 knots, everything. Just in the last two hours we've done seven gybes. The wind was going round in circles. It's back now, though. I'm totally drained. I hope the wind doesn't go higher: I don't want to have to change from the genoa to a smaller headsail. Somehow I've got to rest, but that's so hard because now the breeze has fallen out. We were going OK, but we're not any more. The pilot's just gone off twice, never a good time at the beginning of a twelve-hour stretch of no wind. It really is light. Light variable, 4–7 knots, you can sail with 4–7 knots, but I just can't rest, I can't rest with the pilot going off. I can deal with not going anywhere, but I can't deal with the alarm going off all the time.

DAY SIXTY-NINE 4/02/05
2 days 13 hours ahead
690 miles west of Vigo, Spain

Very stressful last night, very stressful. I had about six hours of absolute hell. We had 4 knots of breeze and were able to sail, and then the breeze would just die for forty-five minutes, spinning round and round and round and round. I furled the genoa and then sat and watched it for forty-five minutes because it was pointless trying to sail. It stabilized for about twenty minutes in one direction at about 3.5 knots, so we could just about get moving, and then it suddenly decided it was going to go through 360 degrees four times, which is obviously quite hard to get sailing in. It finally stabilized after a few hours ESE, and then I could see it coming back up into the north. The bubble of high wasn't as high north as we'd thought but more south-west, and we went right over the top of it, which is why we lost the breeze so early. We're through, though, we're through the high bubble, and we're going to have good light winds for a while. Hopefully there's no second bubble at the same time, so we should be OK. The breeze should come in from the north and then strengthen its arse off, basically! The routeing software wasn't showing that we were going to get very far north, but, as long as the breeze stays where it is, I'm gaining to the north, which is fantastic.

In the end, I duct-taped the alarm up because it was so noisy – I just couldn't bear to hear it any more! But I didn't lose the plot once last night, not even for a second, not in six hours of a complete nightmare. What makes it hard is when you imagine one thing happening and then something very different takes place. You don't know where you are with it, you don't know what's going on, but I never lost it. Yet the night before I couldn't deal with anything, nothing – it's amazing what that sleep difference makes. Three hours yesterday and a few slices during the night. As soon as the winds stabilize, I'll try to sleep some more.

Last night I actually felt hungry, which is a miracle, so around 3.00 a.m. I made my dinner. Your objective is to sleep while the breeze is stable, but you've got to eat as well. I burnt my mouth, as I was shovelling my food down too fast so I would have the chance to sleep even for five minutes! You do what you've got to do to survive. So much of this trip has reflected this basic survival instinct – even down to what you can eat and what you can digest. The only things I remotely want to eat are milk products. I've nearly run out of powdered milk because I've used it all in my tea and on my breakfast cereal. I don't know if it's my body wanting fat because I've had no fat in my diet for the last few months. (Thanks, generator!)

Yesterday a ship passed down my port side – I was on port tack sailing with genoa. There was no blip (on the active echo), no nothing, I didn't see anything. That was quite unnerving, really. Now we're tacking off Finisterre and then heading north – this will take us straight up through the shipping route, so we're going to be on full alert.

I doubt I shall ever be able to express what this trip has put me through, I'm running so close to empty that I believe it's only the energy from others that's keeping me going

Hi, team

I'm sitting here with tears in my eyes, not really knowing what to do with myself. I cannot articulate how I feel; I doubt I shall ever be able to express what this trip has put me through, or continues to put me through ... There have been some incredible moments, but there have also been those moments which are far too painful to bring back ... The hardest part is that I know there is little resilience left ... I'm running so close to empty ...

I'm running so close to empty that I believe it's only the energy from others that's keeping me going. Physically I'm exhausted – not just from the effort of sailing Mobi so hard but also from the constant motion, which makes even standing still impossible. On a scale of 1 to 10 this has been a 9 point something, and I'd stick the Vendée Globe on a 5 max.

To put it briefly, this trip has taken pretty much ALL I have, every last drop and ounce. It has taken everything to get this far – and we're still not there yet. I have never attempted something as hard as this before – I want to tell you now that this will take a long time to recover from ... mentally more than anything else ... though you know that I will be brave and give my return to 'normal' life all I can ... please note that there are NO reserves, and that I'm pretty fragile right now.

I just want you to know how I am inside ... I'm a pretty tough person, but this has taken everything. I chose to do this and I really don't need any sympathy from anyone, quite the reverse, but I do need to know you understand how totally exhausted I really am.

exx

**Yesterday the finish
seemed quite close;
now it feels a very
long way away**

DAY SEVENTY 5/02/05
2 days 6 hours ahead
500 miles west of Cape Finisterre

**It's pretty bad already; it's going to be
a whole lot worse.** The models where
I am now say I should have 18 knots of
breeze, but I've got a 28-knot average
already, gusting 33, and it's not supposed
to get bad for another twelve hours. We're
going to be lucky to come through this

without breaking something or capsizing,
to be frank. The waves are going to be
absolutely huge and we're going to be
going straight across them, which is the
worst thing you could possibly do. I'm
really worried. Just got to keep things
together for the next twenty-four hours.

At the beginning of the night, I managed to get about an hour and a half of sleep because the breeze died. But then I had hours and hours in the night when I couldn't sleep. I was so cold, it's freezing out here, absolutely freezing. I just couldn't get warm, and there were ships around as well. I tell you something, I'm going to be looking forward to sunrise tomorrow morning.

The last hour has been more stable at least – there were a couple of spikes but it is generally OK. I really don't want to bust anything – when the wind went down to 15 knots it was terrible – everything shakes, you're not even loaded and the boat just falls and that's awful. I can't relax at all because it's not a relaxing situation, and it's not like 'Don't worry, you'll be finished in three days,' because right now we're facing the worst conditions from a boat-break point of view that we've had on the entire trip without a doubt.

Yesterday the finish seemed quite close; now it feels a very long way away . . .

DAY SEVENTY-ONE 6/02/05
1 day 23 hours ahead
250 miles WNW of Cape Finisterre

The breeze is still oscillating the whole time. It's so hard to keep the boat going – boat speed at the moment is averaging at 12.7 knots, which is terrible. We had a few really big waves in the night: I was literally thrown out of the bunk by one that broke right over the boat and filled the cockpit – it was lucky I had the door shut. The cuddy was full, everything was awash, all the ropes were swimming around in the cockpit – there must have been a ton of water in there, and I was a bit worried about the structure.

I spent a few hours in my bunk – it was hard, very rough and cold. But, to be honest, it wasn't as cold as the night before. The night before I suffered terribly from the cold.

The last few days of any race or record attempt are always very hard, and this is absolutely no exception

I really worked hard last night – I'm so tired, but I just want to get across the line. It's been a massive project so far, and a lot of energy has gone in from a lot of people. I feel this is the last opportunity to tie the knot – I want to get it right, I want to do it as swiftly and as sweetly as possible. But I'm very tired: I had less than an hour's sleep yesterday night, I've been up all day today, and I'm going to be up all night tonight. I'm just trying to keep things together until we cross that line.

I have absolutely no idea when we're going to cross the finish line. It should be some time tomorrow night. We had 18 knots of breeze an hour ago; we've now got an average of 11 knots. There are some clouds to windward, we've got the tide to contend with, and the breeze is going aft, so there are about four different things that could come into play which could change the fact of me crossing the line some time from midnight to sunrise. I have no idea, it really is a mystery right now – I just want to get there as fast as possible.

I've got the radar alarm going off all the time at the moment. There's always a ship in the area – I'm going to be dealing with ships from now until the finish, including the traffic separation scheme – so that's probably another 12–18 hours of getting round ships.

The last few days of any race or record attempt are always very hard, and this is absolutely no exception. Right now I'm just concentrating on getting to the line as fast as possible.

I know it's going to be a very long night.

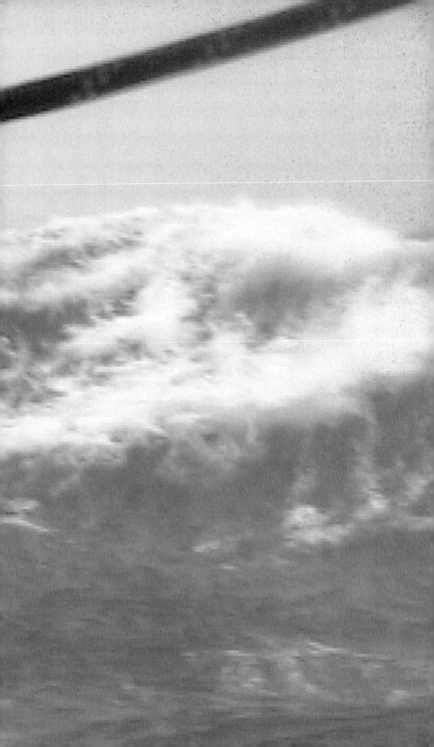

I've got HMS *Liverpool* on my quarter, a light aircraft buzzing me very close and a Royal Navy helicopter just behind me. I need an air traffic controller out here!

DAY SEVENTY-TWO 7/02/05
1 day 8 hours ahead
100 miles to the finish line

It's 11.00 a.m., and the last twenty-four hours have been completely dreadful. We've had everything from full-on gusts of 40 knots to huge seas in the tail end of a storm yesterday. We sailed out of that sea state during the night with some very strong gusts, and we had to tack five

times to get through a small low-pressure system off the north of Spain, which has proved very, very complicated.

There is definitely still a chance to break the record, as long as I don't hit anything or break anything between where I am now and the finish line. I stand a good chance,

but it's going to be, as always, very, very difficult. I was hoping to be in before sunset tonight, but that looks absolutely impossible now. We had a very difficult night last night. I managed only about fifteen minutes of sleep – there were ships everywhere and an exceptionally changeable breeze. It's been a full-on night and I am very, very tired. I've got to get it right. I'm just trying to keep things together until we've crossed that line.

Getting close to land is a strange feeling because it's been a long time since we've even seen any. We didn't see Cape Horn; the islands in the South Atlantic are all that we've seen. There's not been a lot of land sighted from *B&Q*, so the thought of coming back to land is pretty novel in itself. When my brain actually allows itself to relax, then maybe I'll be able to take in what's going on around me.

I can't wait to get in. It's been a very, very long trip and an exceptionally hard one. I'll be glad to be crossing that finish line and finally feeling a little bit of relief.

71 days, 14 hours, 18 minutes and 33 seconds

**When I crossed the line, I felt like
collapsing on the cockpit floor
and just falling asleep.** The pure fact
that you can actually finally let go, that
when you cross the line it's over, it's just
over, and you don't have to worry any
more, that was the biggest emotion –
huge relief. So now I'm elated and at the
same time absolutely drained, it's been a
very tough trip. I've got a mix of emotions
in my mind.

The first real feeling of joy was when
the guys scrambled on board. They had
been following every single step of the
journey, but finally I was home – and they
were there in flesh and blood, right with
me. I've not looked anyone in the eyes for
over two months. Just to be able to see
and touch people again felt so special. To
hug them and share that moment made
the record worth something. Prior to that it
had just seemed one long struggle.

You have to believe you have a chance
when you start on something like this;

When I crossed the line, I felt like collapsing on the cockpit floor and just falling asleep

otherwise you would never have the motivation and drive to build the boat and prepare the boat and to get everything ready. You have to believe that you can do it. I thought Francis's record was beatable – Francis agreed that it was beatable – but to do it the first time, I really didn't think that was possible. It's been a huge challenge, and it's been just a sleigh ride of ups and downs and five-day leads and losing days. I'm very determined when I decide to do something. I will give everything I have to do it. The drive to do that comes from the fact that I work with an unbelievable team, and am supported by some incredible people. And I'm not just out there doing it for me, I'm doing it for everybody. And when the chips are down and things are going wrong, I don't want to let anyone else down, and that's probably one of the biggest motivations.

And now I'm still smiling and I'm on my way home.

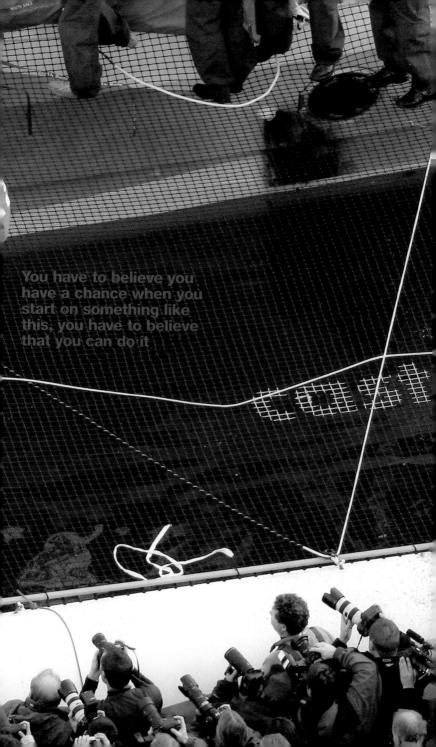

You have to believe you
have a chance when you
start on something like
this, you have to believe
that you can do it

Just to be able to see and touch people again felt so special. To hug them and share that moment made the record worth something

I work with an unbelievable team, and am supported by some incredible people. I'm not just out there doing it for me, I'm doing it for everybody

Ω
OMEGA
OFFICIAL TIMEKEEPER
FOR ELLEN MACARTHUR

HOURS

EPILOGUE

When I climbed off *Kingfisher* at the end of the Vendée Globe four years ago, it was all I could do to prise myself off her. I was distraught; I did not want the story to end. I felt that life was about to change in a big way – and it did.

This time, with *B&Q*, it was different. I was ready to leave her, ready to step off. And it wasn't an intense sadness but a feeling of great joy – the feeling that finally we had done it. Also, more importantly, that the future was still before us. This time I wasn't so scared.

Each of us remembers things that happen in our lives for different reasons. We recall the high points and the low, the joy and the sadness, but there are always things that especially shine out.

There are people involved in this project that have made a huge difference to me, and occasions that have become more than memories. There have been friendships and moments that will shape my life in a far greater way than I could ever have appreciated at the time. However difficult the bad parts were, a smile still comes to my face when I think of the incredible team that I work with, and the energy that they've put into this.

When I look back on the best moments, I see the amazing feeling of teamwork that we all shared. I believe I work with the most passionate, motivated and committed team imaginable. There are few people who really know what it took to make this happen, who are really aware of not just the struggle to break the record but also of the intense preparation that took place over two years. The blood, sweat and tears of these people made the boat what she is today. It was this team that gave her the strength to carry me non-stop around the world.

For however long the record stands, I will never see it as 'my' record. There isn't a shadow of doubt in my mind that it is 'our' record. Although it may have been seen as 'solo' from the outside, the reality is that it was broken not through the efforts of one person but through the work of a collection of very special, dedicated individuals.

That's why when I crossed the finish line I felt nothing other than relief. It was only when I could share what I had achieved with the others that I felt the most intense joy. That was the moment when we had actually done it.

For now, life goes on. Recording those vivid, sometimes beautiful, often painful recollections in this book is perhaps my way of dealing with what happened. I'm turning the page and getting on with things. There are still records to break and races to run.

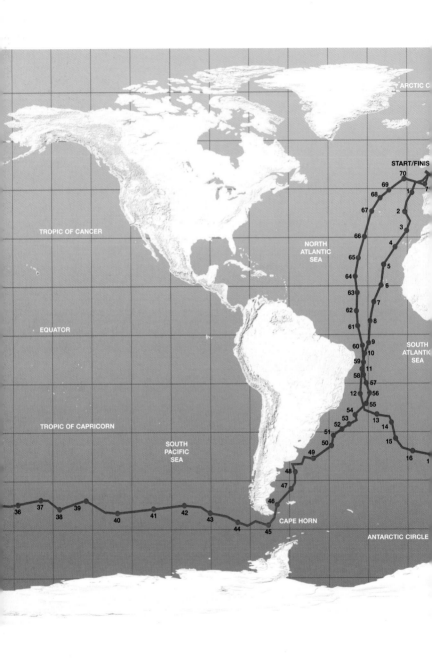

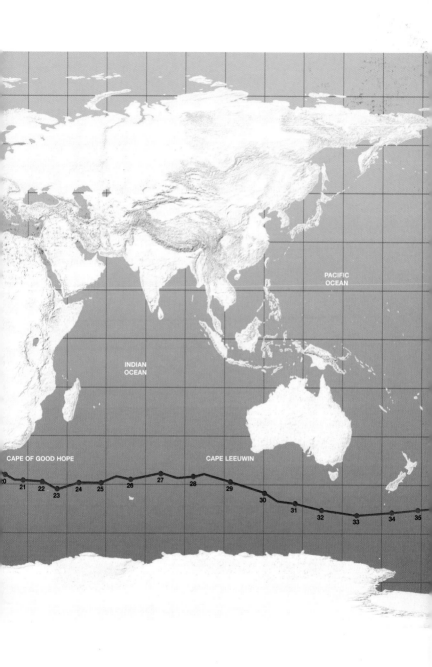

PACIFIC
OCEAN

INDIAN
OCEAN

CAPE OF GOOD HOPE

CAPE LEEUWIN

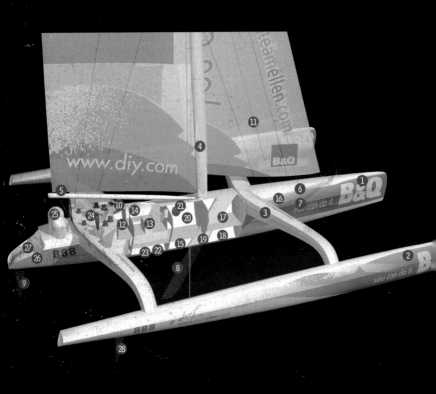

1. Main hull
2. Floats
3. Crossbeams
4. Wingmast
5. Boom
6. Freeboard
7. Chine
8. Centreboard
9. Rudders
10. Cockpit
11. Rigging
12. Cuddy
13. Chart table
14. Bunk and galley area
15. Engine
16. Watertight compartments
17. Sail locker
18. Emergency ballast
19. Foam crash boxes
20. Electronics and generator
21. Escape hatch
22. Fuel tank
23. Water tank
24. Winch systems
25. Satellite domes
26. Sailing trim ballast tank
27. Main rudder and cassette box
28. Float rudders

TECHNICAL SPECIFICATIONS OF B&Q TRIMARAN

Displacement: 8.3 tonnes

Length: 22.9m

Beam: 16.2m

Mast height: 30.6m

Standing rigging: 253.2m

Maximum break tonnes (genoa): 43 tonnes

Main hull surface area: 143.9m²

Main hull internals surface area: 37.29m²

Crossbeams surface area: 51.34 sqm²

Floats surface area: 151.48m²

Floats internal surface area: 35.78m²

Total surface area: 419.79m²

Designers: Nigel Irens/Benoit Cabaret (Nigel Irens Design)

Builders: Boatspeed, Australia

Project management: Offshore Challenges Project

The construction of the 75-foot B&Q trimaran involved six countries in the manufacture of components and hardware:

Australia: build of main hull, floats, beams and fittings

New Zealand: construction of mast and rigging

United Kingdom: construction of rudders, foils and MDF mock-up

United States: construction of 3DL™ sails

France: finishing of 3DL™ sails

Italy: construction of deck hardware

GLOSSARY

active echo – A device that picks up radar signals from other ships and sets off an alarm.

aft – Towards the rear of the boat.

anticyclone – An area of high atmospheric pressure caused by descending air, which becomes warm and dry. Winds radiate from a calm centre, taking a clockwise direction in the northern hemisphere and an anticlockwise direction in the southern hemisphere.

backstay – A stay supporting the mast from the stern.

bilge – The lowest part of the hull that's below the waterline. It collects any water that enters the boat.

bilge pump – A mechanical, electrical or manual pump used to remove water from the bilge.

boom – The spar that extends backwards from the mast base and to which the foot of the mainsail is attached.

bow – The front of the boat.

cabin – A compartment for the crew.

cockpit – An area in the deck from which the boat is steered and the sails are controlled; it's usually located towards the middle or rear of the boat.

Code 0 – An upwind sail known as a gennaker used in light winds.

convergence zone – Where the trade winds of the northern and southern hemispheres converge near the Equator, producing a narrow band of light winds, clouds and thunderstorms (also referred to as ITCZ or Doldrums).

to crack off – To steer away from sailing upwind and therefore to accelerate.

crayons – Slide rods that allow the headboard cars to slide along the mast track.

cuddy – A small sheltered area located between the 'open' cockpit and down below.

daggerboard – A retractable fin that extends vertically from the hull to prevent leeward drift when upwind.

float – Outboard hulls on a trimaran.

fore – Towards the front of the boat.

forestay – A stay supporting the mast from the bow.

furl – To roll up a sail around its stay – a bit like a vertical blind.

furler – The mechanism for rolling a headsail around the forestay.

fuse – A small mechanism fixed between the main rudder and its casing used to hold the main rudder down; fuses are an expendable mechanism that will break if the rudder hits something, allowing the rudder to kick up.

gennaker – A large sail that is a cross between a spinnaker and a genoa.

genoa – A large jib sail that sets in front of the mast but extends aft of the mast.

grib – Files containing weather forecast data.

gybe – To change direction so that the stern passes through the direction of the wind.

halyard – A rope used for raising and lowering sails.

headboard car – A sail is attached to a metal track via a set of 'cars'; the headboard car is the biggest, takes the most load and is the top one in the set.

headsail – Any sail flown forward of the mast used for sailing in upwind conditions (the trimaran has four different headsails that are hoisted on to different forestays). Headsails can be used like gears – the lighter the wind, the bigger the headsail.

high-pressure – *See* anticyclone.

jib – A triangular sail that sets in front of

the mast.

Kevlar™ – A synthetic fibre stronger and lighter than most steels.

knot – A measure of speed equal to one nautical mile (6,076 feet) per hour.

laystock – A vertical linkage in the steering system.

leeward – The direction away from which the wind is coming. Opposite of windward.

low pressure – An area of low atmospheric pressure caused by ascending air; this upward motion means that there is less pressure from the air pushing down on the earth. As air rises, it cools and if there is enough water vapour it may condense to form clouds and rain. Low-pressure systems in the Southern Ocean are especially intense, as they rotate around the globe unstopped by any land mass, gathering immense energy.

luff – The leading edge of the sail; to 'luff up' means to sail closer to the wind when sailing upwind.

mainsail – A large triangular sail that hangs between the mast and the boom.

multihull – Any boat with more than one hull, such as a catamaran or trimaran.

pilot arms – The piston in the autopilot ram.

port – The left side of a boat when one is looking forward.

ram – The driving motor for the autopilot.

to reach – Sailing with the wind perpendicular to the side of the boat.

reef – The section of the sail that can be reduced – a mainsail can normally be 'reefed' three times over by gathering the excess sail of the reef section along the boom.

ridge – An elongated area of high pressure in the atmosphere.

rudder – A vertical fin at the stern for steering a boat. It is designed to flip up 90 degrees if it collides with anything.

rudder cassette box – The pivoting box that the rudder sits in.

runner – Adjustable aft stay used to control tension on the mast.

seamount – An underwater mountain whose peak lies below the surface of the ocean.

sheet – A rope used to control the sails.

solent – The intermediate fore sail, between the staysail and the genoa.

speedo – Measurement instrument for boat speed.

squall – A sudden intense wind storm of short duration, often accompanied by rain. Squalls frequently accompany an advancing cold front.

starboard – The right side of a boat when one is looking forward.

stay – Lines running fore and aft down from the top of the mast to keep the mast upright. Also used to carry some sails. The backstay is aft of the mast, and the forestay is forward of the mast.

staysail – A triangular sail similar to, but smaller than, the jib.

stern – The rear of the boat.

storm jib – A very small, strong sail used in rough conditions (the smallest front sail in the sail inventory).

tack – The direction in which the boat is sailing in relation to the wind, or to change the direction of the boat by turning the bow through the wind; also, the lowest front corner of a sail.

tiller – A bar or handle attached to the rudder and used to steer the boat.

trade winds – Persistent tropical winds that blow from the subtropical high-pressure centres towards the equatorial low.

trim – The fore and aft balance of a boat.

trimaran – A three-hulled boat.

windward – Towards the direction from which the wind is coming.

wing mast – Mast shaped like an aerofoil section, which is similar to an aeroplane wing.

PICTURE CREDITS

The publishers and author are grateful to the following for permission to reproduce photographs and sketches. Every effort has been made to trace copyright holders. The publishers will be glad to rectify in future editions any errors or omissions brought to their attention.

Reproduced from original sketches, with kind permission by Nigel Irens: pp. 14–15

Benoit Stichelbaut/DPPI: pp. 2–5; 30–31; 40–41; 60–61; 68; 69; 72–3; 92–3; 100–101; 103; 113; 134–5; 138–9; 162–3; 180; 181; 183; 184–5; 216–17; 232; 233; 234; 238–9; 240; 244–5; 246–7

Jacques Vapillon/DPPI: pp. 26–7; 28–9; 36–7; 43; 59; 62; 82–3; 110–11; 142; 144–5; 164–6; 188–9; 190–91; 204–7; 258–9; 266

Liot Vapillon/DPPI: pp. 10–11; 264; 265; 267; 268–9; 270; 271; top 272; 273; 274; 287

Vincent Curuchet/DPPI: pp. 33; 66–7; 70; 76–7; 114–15; 124–5; 130–31; 146–7; 170–71; 186–7; 199; 200; 202–3; 208–9; 231; 242

Andrea Francolini/DPPI: pp. 16; bottom left 17; 44

David Richard/DPPI: bottom p. 18

Carlo Borlenghi/DPPI: pp. 260–61

Jean Marie Liot/DPPI: pp. 20–21; 22–3; 24–5; 35; 56–7; 249

Jon Nash/DPPI: pp. 78; 80–81

Billy Black/DPPI: pp. 74–5; 152

Omega/DPPI: pp. 276–7

Royal Navy/DPPI: p. 52

Ellen MacArthur/DPPI: pp. 38–9; 49; 53; 55; 90; 98; 133; 140–41; 168; 210; 212; 220–21; 223; 236–7

Mark Lloyd: pp. 262–3; bottom 272; 279

Crown Copyright/MOD. Reproduced with the permission of the Controller of Her Majesty's Stationery Office: pp. 46; 213; 256–7

Thierry Martinez: pp. 48; 50–51; 214–15

Peter Favelle/Alamy: pp. 150–51

1435 Flight, RAF Tornadoes, Falklands: pp. 192; 193

Onne van der Wal/Bluegreen Pictures: pp. 194–5

Jason Edwards/Getty Images: pp.196–7

Bildagentur Franz Waldhaeusl/Alamy: pp. 224–5

Cartesia/Getty Images: pp. 280–81

The remaining pictures are reproduced with kind permission of Ellen MacArthur/Offshore Challenges Sailing Group

A Note on the Pictures

The grainy, lined appearance of a number of the pictures used in *Race Against Time* is because they were captured from video shot during the race.

ACKNOWLEDGEMENTS

The acknowledgements should form a book in their own right.

As the project took shape and developed, the number of people involved grew and grew. Each and every person that worked on it has their own story, from those who built her to those who helped prepare her to sail. You are all responsible in your own way for the record, and I really hope that you all feel that. Mark, if I had not met you in January 1996, I am sure that none of this would have happened. You've always been there for me at sea and on land – our incredible journey continues.

But I'd like to finish by thanking the longest-suffering of you all, and that's my family. Had my parents not given their children the freedom to follow their dreams, I would never even have set foot on a boat. Mum, Dad – the whole family – you are the most important thing in my life. I love you all so much.

ellen x

FOLLOW THE PROJECT WITH THE  offshore challenges
sailing team

It doesn't have to stop here ... When Ellen and her Offshore Challenges Sailing Team are out racing, her support team in collaboration with her title sponsors, DIY retailers B&Q and Castorama, communicate her project to thousands of people all over the world via email and SMS updates.

If you would like to receive these updates please sign up at: htpp://www.teamellen.com/updates.asp
Updates can be sent daily, weekly or just when there is major news.

 THE ELLEN MACARTHUR TRUST

Launched in January 2003, the Ellen MacArthur Trust was set up to enliven and empower the lives of children suffering or recovering from cancer or leukaemia. The main activity of the Trust involves taking the kids out sailing around the south coast of the UK. 'Meeting the challenge of sailing at sea, the children gain confidence and are reminded that there is life beyond their illness. At the same time they meet friends suffering from the same disease, which reminds them they are not alone in their struggle.'
For more information please log on to: http://www.ellenmacarthurtrust.org or email: info@ellenmacarthurtrust.org

---

Don't forget you can follow Ellen's amazing stories on DVD as well; you can buy these DVDs online at http://www.ellenmacarthur.com or by completing the form below. This form entitles you to a 10 per cent discount. Please send the completed form and payment to: Offshore Challenges, Cowes Waterfront – Venture Quays, Castle Street, East Cowes, Isle of Wight, PO32 6EZ

☐ I would like to buy __ copies of **The Ellen MacArthur Story Part 1** – Relive Ellen's adventures in the Vendée Globe, Route Du Rhum and Jules Verne attempt on DVD at £16.99 inc. VAT

☐ I would like to buy __ copies of **The Official Record Breaking Story** – Follow Ellen's epic solo round the world record on this exciting new DVD at £19.95 inc. VAT
Please add £1.50 p&p in the UK, £2.00 for the European mainland, and £2.50 for elsewhere per order.

☐ I enclose a cheque made payable to 'Offshore Challenge Ltd' for _____
☐ I authorize payment on my Credit Card as follows

Name on Card:
Address for Card:

Type of card: (VISA) (MASTERCARD)
Card Number:
Expiry Date: Signature:
Address for delivery if different from above:

Email address:
Phone Number:

Offshore Challenge Ltd is registered under the Data Protection Act 1998